WOOL FELTING
WORKSHOP

WOOL FELTING WORKSHOP

Vivian Peritts

STERLING

New York / London
www.sterlingpublishing.com

Prolific Impressions Production Staff:
Editor in Chief: Mickey Baskett
Copy Editor: Phyllis Mueller
Graphics: Cindy Gorder
Styling: Lenos Key
Photography: Jerry Mucklow, Joel Tressler
Administration: Jim Baskett

STERLING and the distinctive Sterling logo are registered trademarks of Sterling Publishing Co., Inc.

Library of Congress Cataloging-in-Publication Data

Peritts, Vivian.
  Wool felting workshop / Vivian Peritts.
    p. cm.
  Includes index.
  ISBN: 978-1-4027-4432-7
  1. Felt work. 2. Felting. 3. Clothing and dress—Remaking. I. Title.

TT849.5.P48 2008
746'.0463—dc22   2007038268

10 9 8 7 6 5 4 3 2 1

Published by Sterling Publishing Co., Inc.
387 Park Avenue South, New York, NY 10016
© 2008 by Prolific Impressions, Inc.
Distributed in Canada by Sterling Publishing
c/o Canadian Manda Group, 165 Dufferin Street,
Toronto, Ontario, Canada M6K 3H6
Distributed in the United Kingdom by GMC Distribution Services,
Castle Place, 166 High Street, Lewes, East Sussex, England BN7 1XU
Distributed in Australia by Capricorn Link (Australia) Pty. Ltd.
P.O. Box 704, Windsor, NSW 2756, Australia

Printed in China
All rights reserved

Sterling ISBN 978-1-4027-4432-7

For information about custom editions, special sales, premium and corporate purchases, please contact Sterling Special Sales Department at 800-805-5489 or specialsales@sterlingpublishing.com.

About the Author

Vivian Peritts is a designer and crafter who has written several books and created over 100 patterns. Her designs have appeared in numerous national publications. She has taught many workshops at national trade shows and has been a frequent guest on national cable television programs.

She lives in Marietta, Georgia with her husband, Virgil, two dogs, and a parrot.

Acknowledgments

Vivian Peritts thanks Linda Baird for all her help in preparing the manuscript. She also thanks the following for their generous contributions of products for use in this book:

For Ultra Solvy™ Heavy Water Soluble Stabilizer and Thread:
Sulky of America, 3113 Broadpoint Drive, Punta Gorda, FL 33983 USA
www.sulky.com

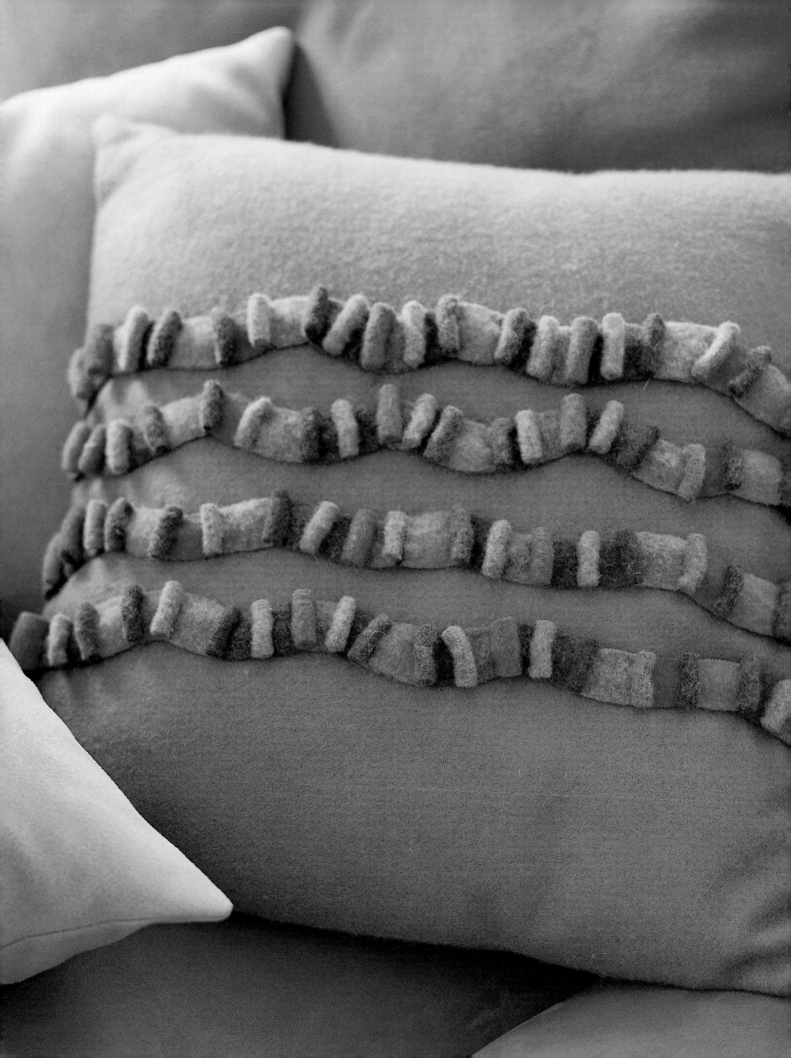

Table of Contents

About the Author 5

Introduction: Creative Recycling 9

Supplies to Get Started 10

   Wool Sweaters Become Felted Wool 11

   Cutting Tools 12

   Sewing Tools & Supplies 13

   Needles for Hand Sewing 14

   Embellishments 14

   Yarns & Threads 15

   Beads & Beading Wire 15

   Miscellaneous Supplies 16

Basic Techniques 17

   Creating Felted Wool 18

   Cutting & Sewing 19

   Finishing Edges 21

   Decorative Embroidery Stitches . . . 21

Felted Wool Projects 23

   Primrose Path Throw 24

   Pink Fringed Pillow 28

   Nine-Dot Pillow 30

   Circles of Cuffs Pillow 31

   Loopy Stripes Pillow 32

   32 Squares Pillow 24

   Crazy Quilt Trunk Top 36

   Purple Flower Stool 38

   Reupholstered Round Ottoman . . . 42

   Appliqued Chair Cover 46

   Chair Seat Cushion 50

   Monogrammed Chair Cover 51

   Flower Cuts Rug 52

31

42

64

106

114

Appliqued Placemat 58

Coiled Oval Rug 60

Scalloped Edge Rug 62

Sweet Dreams Baby Blanket 64

Heart Hot Water Bottle Cover 70

Lamb Hot Water Bottle Cover 72

Cuddly Brown Bear 76

Boo Boo Toy 80

Penguin Pal 82

Personalized Toy Crate 86

Initial Tote 90

Dowel Trivet 93

Round Dog Bed 94

Tea Cozy & Teapot Mat 96

Leaves & Petals Table Runner 98

Bull's Eye Trivet 102

Striped Pot Handle Cover 103

Orange Pot Handle Cover 104

Fish Pot Handle Cover 106

Paisley Pot Holder 110

Circles Pot Holder 112

Four Patch Pot Holder 113

Brown Bag It 114

Striped Tassel 116

Gray & Green Tassel 117

Utility Bin Cover 118

Utility Bin Label Holder 120

Flower Label Holder 122

Diaper Applique 124

Metric Conversion Chart 126

Index 127

Make Wool Felted Projects for Your Home with Creative Recycling

Wool felting is many times called "boiled wool." When I did some research about what felted wool was and how it was done, I decided to experiment with my old sweaters. So I washed them and dried them. When I took that first wool sweater out of the clothes dryer I knew I had the beginnings of something exciting. I had created felted wool fabric—fabric I could use to make all kinds of new and interesting home accessories and gifts. Discovering I could "boil" old wool sweaters to create this felted wool was one of those "wow" moments for me. I realized I could recycle old wool sweaters, save money, and be creative all at the same time.

Don't throw those old wool sweaters away—recycle them! Why not take all those wonderful woolen memories and combine them into new items for your home. This book is filled with ideas for recycling and reusing your (or someone else's) castoff wool sweaters, old wool clothes, and woolen fabric by turning them into felted woolen fabric and cutting and combining them in interesting ways.

You'll learn everything you need to get started, including how to select sweaters for recycling and a simple technique for felting. You'll see piecing and cutting techniques for felted sweaters, machine and hand embroidery for stitching and embellishing, and sewing techniques for felted fabric.

This book is stuffed full of projects you can make for your home—more than 40 in all. There are cozy throws and blankets, decorative pillows, coverings for chairs and stools and ottomans—even a dog bed. There are one-of-a-kind creations such as charming stuffed animals and toys, a personalized toy chest, and a monogrammed tote. Practical items such as tabletop accessories like placemats, a table runner, and trivets, plus a tea cozy and pot holders for the kitchen are fun to make and use. And who would have thought you could make such gorgeous rugs from an old knit sweater! You find such a wide variety of useful, wonderful, colorful, and fun to make projects that are also fun to give as gifts. — Vivian Peritts

Supplies to Get Started

*T*his section shows and describes the supplies and tools you'll need to create your felted wool projects. You'll start with wool sweaters and learn how to make the wool fabric you'll need for the projects. I'll also explain the basic sewing tools and the specialized tools and materials you'll need for trimming and embellishing.

Wool Sweaters Become Felted Wool

Start with a knitted sweater–100% wool is best to create the felted wool fabric. Start your search for sweaters in your own closets and storage areas. Chances are you have sweaters you or other family members have outgrown. Or sweaters that are stained or torn or damaged by moths. This is your chance to recycle them and use them again.

Thrift shops are the next best place to look for sweaters for felting–you'll find them in every shape, color, and size. They're inexpensive (a few dollars each) so go ahead and buy a lot of them–you'll have lots of material for your projects. You'll be giving these sweaters a second life and recycling something that might otherwise be discarded, and your purchases benefit the charities.

Since size doesn't matter, check out men's and children's sweaters as well. Choose sweaters in colors you love. Sweaters with knitted patterns, wool embroidery, and multi-colored designs like stripes and argyles can add interest and texture. Don't overlook sweaters with holes in them. (I call these "openings of opportunity".) If the color is too good to pass up,

you can work around the holes. Small holes will disappear in the felting process, and you can mend larger holes with wool yarn before felting or simply cut around them.

I have used knitted wool sweaters to make most of the projects in this book, but you can also felt 100% woven wool fabric and dry-clean only garments or use "boiled wool" fabrics or jackets. Boiled wool is what its name implies–wool that has been shrunk by hot water. Use the same felting process for wool fabric and boiled wool that you use for sweaters.

- Choose 100% wool sweaters. Avoid blends.

- Choose sweaters and fabrics labeled "Dry Clean Only."

- If a garment has appliques or embroidery, check to see if those are 100% wool as well. If they aren't, remove them before felting.

This shows sweater before and after washing and drying. The fibers mat together, get denser, causing the overall garment to become smaller.

Cutting Tools

SCISSORS

• **Fabric scissors** with sharp blades make precise, clean-edged cuts—even through multiple layers. Scissors with longer blades provide more efficient cutting; shorter blades provide more control. Contoured offset handles reduce hand fatigue and make cutting easier on flat surfaces. Choose a pair that feels good in your hand; for additional comfort, try a pair with padded handles.

• **Small craft scissors** are useful for snipping threads and yarns and for precise cutting in tight areas, such as trimming close to stitching after joining fabrics with machine embroidery. Their small size provides more control.

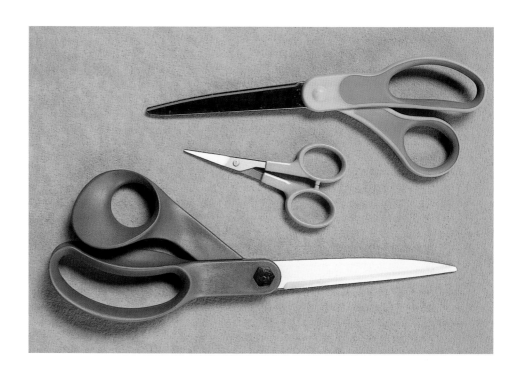

ROTARY CUTTERS

Rotary cutters make cutting fabric easy and fast. They have a sharp metal wheel for cutting that is mounted on a plastic handle. They can cut thick and thin fabrics and make straight or curved cuts. When the blade becomes dull, it can be replaced. Rotary cutters come in different sizes. Choose one that feels comfortable in your hand.

CUTTING MAT

A self-healing cutting mat to protect your work surface when you use rotary cutters is a must. It's a good idea to buy the largest one you can afford.

RULER

Use a ruler when cutting with rotary cutters for cutting straight, precise lines. A transparent one will allow you to see the fabric as you cut, and the markings will allow you to align the ruler with markings on the fabric or on your cutting mat.

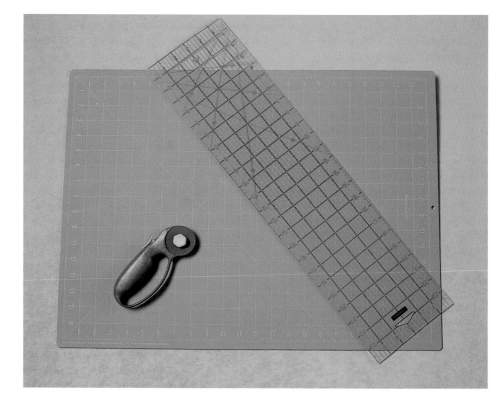

Sewing Tools & Supplies

SEWING MACHINE

Although many projects can be created with hand stitches, machine stitching is the quickest, easiest way to piece the sections of felted wool to create a larger piece of fabric, to sew seams, and add decorative stitching.

Machine stitches that give the best results are overlock stitches. Most machines can make some form of an overlock stitch. I like to use a 1/4" seam allowance for most seams, and I use overlock stitches for joining overlapped pieces of wool. If your machine doesn't have an overlock stitch, use a zig-zag stitch.

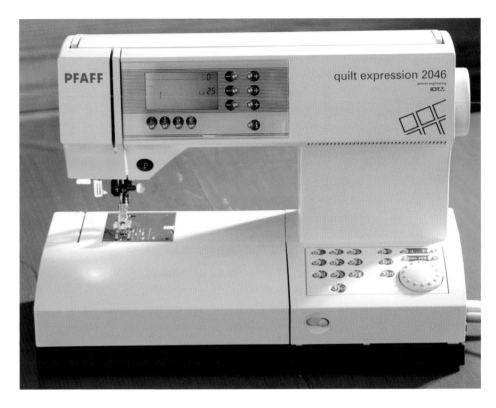

THREAD

Regular sewing thread–the kind that comes on spools in a huge variety of colors–is readily available at fabric, crafts, and department stores. Use it for machine stitching and hand sewing tasks such as attaching trims and buttons.

FABRIC STABILIZER

When machine stitching felted wool, I always use a stabilizer to help keep the fabric from stretching out of shape. A water soluble (rinse-away) stabilizer keeps the wool from stretching out of shape as you stitch and is easy to remove. It comes in packages, rolls, and bolts in various widths and lengths. Follow the manufacturer's instructions for best results.

SEAM RIPPER

You'll want to have a seam ripper to remove unwanted stitching from garments, to remove buttons from sweaters, and to remove unwanted trims from sweaters before felting.

TAPE MEASURE

A tape measure is indispensable for measuring curved surfaces and curved areas of patterns. Choose one made of a material that won't stretch out of shape.

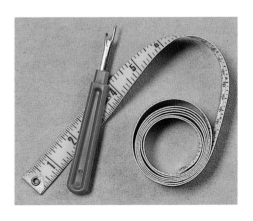

Needles for Hand Sewing

Hand sewing needles are used for basting, embroidery, and beading and for attaching buttons and trims. Choose needles for hand sewing according to the task.

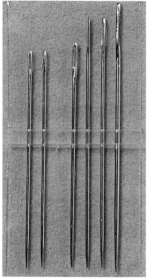

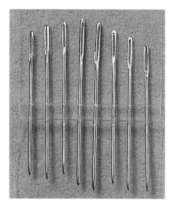

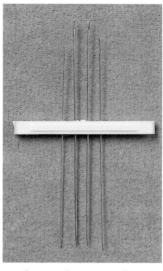

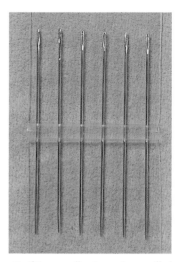

Darners are long, heavy needles with large eyes that are used for stitching with yarn. Used for finishing edges with yarn, ribbon and floss.

Tapestry needles have large eyes and blunt points that allow the needle to pass easily between the yarns in the fabric so they are ideal for stitching on knitted items. Great for doing embroidery with yarns and floss.

Beading needles are very fine needles used for sewing beads, sequins, and pearls.

Quilting needles (sometimes called *basting* needles) are long, fine needles that are good for sewing through multiple layers of fabric.

Embellishments

BEADS & BEADING WIRE

Beads add color, texture, and sparkle, and they look great when combined with felted wool. Beads can be sewn with thread or strung on wire. The individual projects contain specific instructions for using beads.

Embellishments, continued

BUTTONS

Buttons come in a huge variety of designs, materials, colors, and textures. They can be used as closures, as accents, and as decorations.

Yarns & Threads

WOOL YARNS

Wool yarns can be used for decoration before or after felting. If added before felting, the yarn will shrink along with the sweater.

Tapestry or Persian yarn is 3-ply 100% wool yarn that is used mainly for crewel embroidery and needlepoint. Find it in needlework stores in skeins of various lengths.

KNITTING YARN

Use 100% wool **knitting yarn** for knitting and crocheting. Find it in needlework stores and craft departments. Decorative yarns of all types can be used for embellishing felted wool and for adding interest, color, and texture. The yarns can be of any size or fiber content, and they can be textured, string, or ribbon yarns. Many are great for edging. Some are too bulky to pull through the wool but are wonderful for couching (attaching) on the surface with machine or by hand stitches. (See the Basic Techniques section for instructions.)

Wool yarns

Knitting yarns

EMBROIDERY FLOSS

Floss is 6-ply cotton thread that comes in a pull skein in a huge range of colors. I also use **pearl (perle) cotton** embroidery thread, which comes in skeins or on balls. I use this for some decorative stitches and trims.

15

Miscellaneous Supplies

MARKING PENS & PENCILS

Marking pens and pencils are used to mark the placement of decorative yarns and trims before stitching and to mark the placement of buttons and trims. You can also use markers to trace around pattern pieces. Choose chalk or water soluble markers, which make removable marks, for areas where you don't want the marks to show.

TRANSFER PAPER

Use transfer paper for transferring pattern markings and pattern details for embroidery.

PATTERNS

All the patterns you need to make the projects in this book are included. Some—the smaller pieces—are presented full size; patterns for larger pieces can be traced and enlarged. The percentage for enlarging is noted on the pattern.

NEEDLENOSE PLIERS

Needlenose pliers are great for bending, shaping, and twisting wire. Pliers with spring action handles are self-opening and reduce hand fatigue; ones with coated handles are easier to grip.

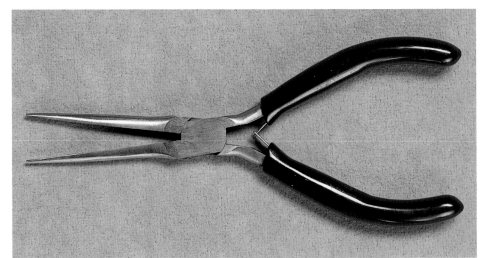

Basic
Techniques

You will learn the basic techniques for felting of the sweaters, cutting the wool, and how to create larger pieces of fabric. Included are techniques for finishing edges and creating hand or machine embroidery for decorating your projects.

Creating Felted Wool

You may have made felted wool before, though perhaps not intentionally. (Remember accidentally putting a wool garment through the washer and dryer and pulling out something smaller and denser?) Felting sweaters works much the same way. The intentional method of felting I found to be most effective is very simple. You need a regular washing machine, a clothes dryer, and some dishwashing soap or shampoo. Because the projects in this book are made by cutting up felted wool sweaters or felted wool fabric, there is no sizing or blocking involved.

Wool felting occurs when hot water and soap such as liquid dishwashing soap or shampoo are combined with the agitating action of a washing machine. Wool fibers naturally have barbs that intertwine and catch on each other; heat, soap, and friction from agitation cause the fibers to become more intertwined, making the sweater or piece of fabric smaller and more compact and dense. How a sweater will *felt* depends on the size of yarn it was made with and the stitches used.

STEP 1: WASH

Place one or two sweaters or pieces of wool fabric in a washing machine set on the lowest water level. Because agitation and friction are important to the felting process, it's a good idea to felt more than one item at a time to increase the friction. Add hot water and one tablespoon of liquid dishwashing soap or shampoo. Wash.

TIP: If you only have one item to felt, throw in an old towel or a few old t-shirts to create more friction

STEP 2: DRY

After the washing and spinning cycles are finished, place the sweaters or fabric in a dryer set on high heat and tumble until dry. *Note: Some felters prefer to air dry their felted wool, rather than using the dryer. Honestly, I can't tell the difference.* I use the dryer because I typically felt many sweaters at one time, and I don't have enough flat surfaces to lay them on. Repeat the process to shrink the sweater even more. The more you do this, the bulkier the wool becomes. Successful felting has occurred when the knitting stitches in the garment are no longer visible.

A sweater before and after washing and drying.

Cutting & Sewing

CUTTING

Decide which sections of your felted sweaters or fabric you want to use for your project. Cut open the sides of the sweater to flatten the fabric as much as possible, and cut away the ribbed collar, cuffs, and bottom if they are not going to be part of the project. Cut the knits into pieces, following the individual project instructions. Use a rotary cutter and a straight edge for straight cuts, working on top of a self-healing cutting mat for best results. This method will give you the smoothest and straightest edges. Cut curved pieces with sharp fabric scissors.

Using the patterns in this book, determine the sizes of fabric pieces needed to create your project. Sometimes you can get a large enough piece from a sweater, other times you may need to sew pieces of fabric together to make a piece large enough to construct your project.

CUTTING LONG STRIPS

When you need a long strip of fabric, you can cut the sweater into a spiral to achieve this. Choose a pullover sweater that does not have side seams.

Here's how:

1. Cut off the ribbing at the bottom of the sweater. Set it aside. (Fig. 1)
2. Decide how wide you want the strip to be and cut straight up from the bottom of the sweater. For example, if you decide you want a strip 1/2" wide, cut 1/2" up from the bottom. (Fig. 1)
3. Begin cutting around the bottom of the sweater. Continue cutting, spiraling upward, keeping the strip the same width, until you have a strip as long as you need for your project. Trim the irregular shape at the beginning of your strip. (Fig. 2) ✳

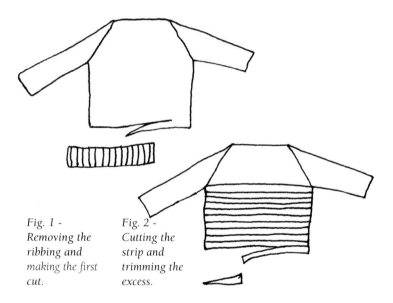

Fig. 1 - Removing the ribbing and *making the first cut.*

Fig. 2 - *Cutting the strip and trimming the excess.*

SEWING FELTED WOOL FABRIC

Always use a stabilizer when sewing a seam or when joining two pieces of felted wool together by sewing machine. A rinse away stabilizer works well–it keeps the wool from stretching and is easy to remove.

An overlock stitch works well for sewing felted fabric; most machines make some type of overlock stitch. I use overlock stitches for making narrow seams (1/4" from the outer edge) and for joining overlapped pieces of wool. If your machine doesn't make an overlock stitch, use a zig-zag stitch.

continued on page 20

Cutting & Sewing, continued

MAKING LARGER PIECES OF FABRIC

1. Layout the pieces of felted wool, overlapping them 3/8". Pin pieces together. Continue adding pieces until you have the size of piece needed. Use your pattern piece as a guide for the size and shape of pieced fabric needed. (Photo 1)

2. Sew the pieces together with a sewing machine, using a decorative stitch. (Photo 2 & 3)

3. When you have sewn the pieces together, lay the pattern piece on the fabric and trim to shape of pattern. (Photo 4)

Photo 1: Pinning cut pieces together.

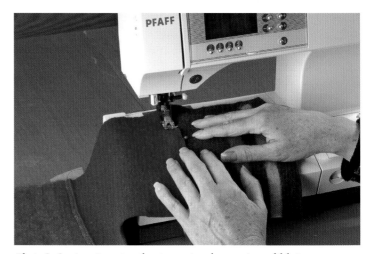

Photo 4. Pattern piece is placed on fabric and cut to size.

Photo 3. Pieces are joined with a decorative stitch, using stabilizer under the seam.

Photo 2: Sewing pieces together to create a larger piece of fabric.

MAKING RAW SEAM JOINS

Many of the projects in this book use the technique of having the raw seams on the outside of the project. This creates an interesting, casual look that is popular in both fashion and home decorating items. To do this, pin the wool fabric pattern pieces together, with **wrong sides** together. Use a sewing machine to stitch the pieces together. Seams will not ravel on felted wool.

Finishing Edges

After the felting has occurred, the sweater can be cut easily with scissors, and the edges will not fray or unravel. Pinking shears can be used for cutting but are not necessary. Much of the time I leave edges unfinished, but hand stitching can be used to add another decorative element. Here are two hand stitches I often use for finishing edges.

OVERCAST STITCH

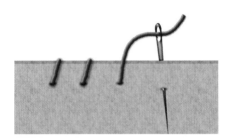

Keep the stitches evenly spaced, approximately 1/2" apart and 1/2" long.

BLANKET STITCH

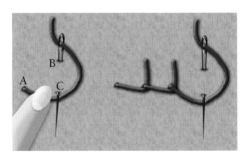

Work this stitch from left to right, keeping your stitches the same distance apart. Come up at A, hold the thread with your thumb, go down at B, and come up at C, bringing the needle tip over the thread. Carefully pull the thread into place. The bottom of the stitch will lie on the edge.

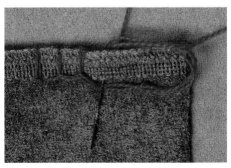

Decorative Embroidery Stitches

MACHINE EMBROIDERY

Machine embroidery stitches can be used for piecing the fabric together or for decoration. I use a water soluble stabilizer when I machine stitch.

Here the machine stitches are shown done on paper so that you can see them better.

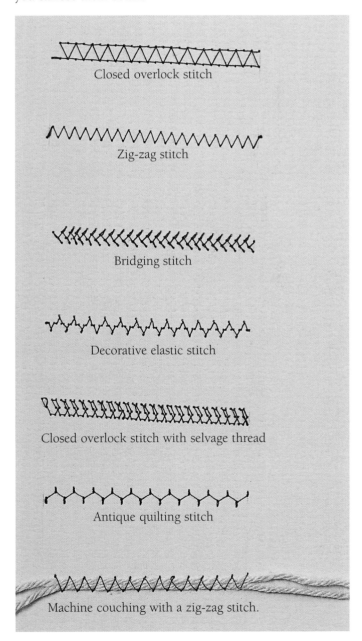

Closed overlock stitch

Zig-zag stitch

Bridging stitch

Decorative elastic stitch

Closed overlock stitch with selvage thread

Antique quilting stitch

Machine couching with a zig-zag stitch.

continued on page 22

Decorative Embroidery Stitches, continued

HAND EMBROIDERY

I often use hand embroidery stitches for embellishing. It is not necessary to use stabilizer when hand stitching felted wool. In addition to the stitches below, you can use the overcast stitch and blanket stitch, described and shown on the preceding page.

CHAIN STITCH

1. Come up at A. Go down to the left of A and come up at B.

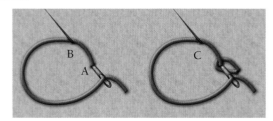

Loop the thread under the needle point from right to left.

2. Pull the thread through. Go down to the left of B, inserting the needle through the loop, and come up at C. Loop thread as shown in step 1.

FRENCH KNOT

Come up at A with the needle tip pointing toward your left arm and wrap the thread four

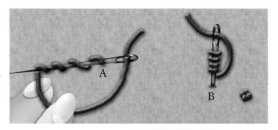

times around the needle. While holding the thread taut, turn the needle toward you, taking the

needle down at B as close as you can to A. Guide the thread into the fabric and hold the knot in place until your needle is all the way through the fabric.

SATIN STITCH

Put the needle in at A and come out at B. Pull the thread gently. Place the stitches close together, continuing to go down and come up. Keep an even edge and keep the tension tight but smooth.

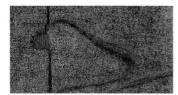

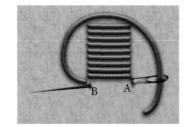

SINGLE CROSS STITCH

Come up at A, down at B, up at C, down at D. The stitch can be reversed so that top half slants from lower right to upper left.

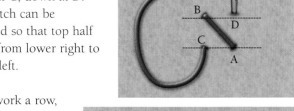

1. To work a row, make even, equally spaced diagonal stitches, working from bottom to top. Then go down at top left of previous stitch to work back across row.

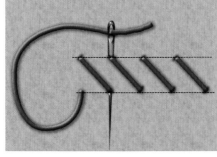

2. Continue in same manner, slanting stitches in opposite direction to form line of crosses.

STEM STITCH or OUTLINE STITCH

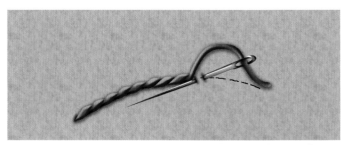

Working from left to right, bring the needle up at the end of the line to be covered. Insert the needle point a short distance ahead, bringing the point out halfway between the place of insertion and the starting place.

Felted Wool Projects

*I*t's time to get started! On the following pages, you'll find instructions for a variety of projects–more than 40 in all–throws and decorative pillows, coverings for chairs and stools and ottomans–even a dog bed. Gorgeous rugs and handy storage containers. Things especially for kids, such as cuddly stuffed animals and toys, a personalized toy chest, and a baby blanket. You'll also find tabletop accessories like placemats, a table runner, and trivets, plus a tea cozy and pot holders for the kitchen. Useful, wonderful, colorful one-of-a-kind creations.

Primrose Path Throw

Colorful flowers and leaves form a border on the perimeter of a pieced throw composed of felted gray, charcoal, and black sweaters. Because you will want to cuddle up with this throw, choose cashmere and other soft knitted wools.

Finished size: 50" X 50"

SUPPLIES

Felted Wool:
- Assorted sweaters in blacks and grays (for the base)
- Assorted sweater sleeves in bright floral colors and stripes (for the flowers)
- Assorted shades of green pieces (for the leaves)

Other Supplies:
- Wool fettuccine-shaped yarn in browns and greens (for the vine)
- Wool multi-colored yarn (for the leaf veins)
- Water soluble stabilizer
- Black sewing thread
- Sewing machine

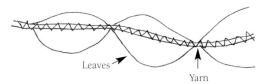
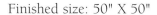

Leaves

Yarn

Fig. 1 - Making the leaf string.

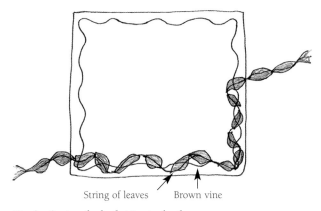

String of leaves   Brown vine

Fig. 2 - Sewing the leaf string to the throw.

INSTRUCTIONS

Make the Base:
1. Overlap pieces of black and gray wool and sew them into a piece 50" X 50" (or your desired size). Use an overlock stitch on all overlaps, and use stabilizer under the fabric.
2. When you have pieced the base, trim the sides as needed to square up the shape.
3. Remove the stabilizer by washing the base and drying it in the dryer.

Add the Flower-and-Leaf Border:
Note: You don't need to use stabilizer on the border.
1. Use a zig-zag stitch to apply the fettuccine-shaped brown-and-green yarn to look like a wavy vine around the edges.
2. Using the patterns provided as guides, cut assorted leaf shapes from green felted wool. TIP: Cut each one separately so they don't all look alike.
3. Place the thinner multi-color yarn on the top of a leaf like a vein. Stitch the yarn to the leaf using a zig-zag stitch. Do not cut thread, but continue adding leaves, to make the string of leaves. See Fig. 1.
4. Zig-zag stitch the string of leaves to the edge of the throw, placing the leaves so they criss-cross the vine but don't entirely cover it. See Fig. 2.
5. For the flowers, cut 3/4" wide rings from felted striped sweater sleeves. Gather one edge of each ring and pull tightly to form the flowers. Note in the photo how the different-color stripes form the flower centers.
6. Sew the flowers individually along the leaf vine, clustering two together in some places for variety ✳

Patterns for Primrose Path Throw

Actual size

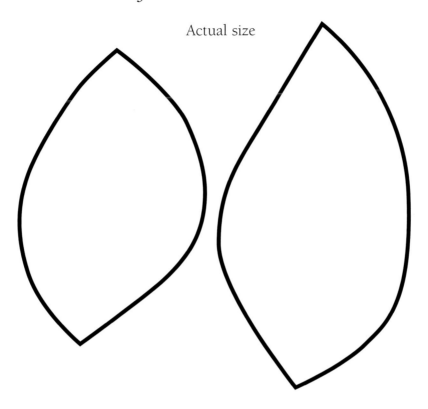

Pattern for Pink Fringed Pillow

Actual size
Cut 5
Instructions on page 28

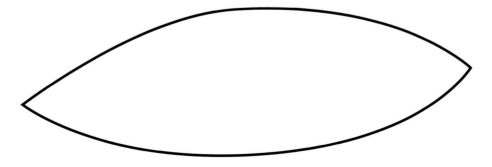

Pink Fringed Pillow

This pink pillow has a flap closure like a purse. The flap is trimmed with a felted wool fringe and accented with a cluster of multi-colored flowers and leaves.

Finished size: 18" x 12"

SUPPLIES

Felted Wool:
- Pink sweater (for the pillow base)
- Sweater sleeves in floral colors and stripes (for the flowers)
- Green sweater pieces (for the leaves)
- Orange sweater (for the fringe)

Other Supplies:
- Pillow form, 10" x 16"
- Sewing thread - White, black, orange
- Sewing machine

INSTRUCTIONS

Cut:
1. From the pink felted wool, cut two pieces, each 19" x 12-1/2", for the front and back of the pillow.
2. Also from the pink wool, cut a piece for the flap 19" x 6-1/2". On one long side, round off both corners to form a curve. See Fig 1.
3. Cut a 25" x 1-1/2" strip of orange wool. Cut a 1/4" wide fringe 1" deep all along one side of the strip.
4. From the ribbing on the ends of the sweater sleeves, cut two rings, each 2" wide. (In the project photo, these are the red and orange flower buds.)
5. From the striped parts of the sweater

sleeves, cut two rings, each 2" wide. (In the project photo, these are the multi-colored flowers–one is open, the other is a bud.)
6. Cut five leaves from green wool, using the pattern provided.

Sew:
1. Sew the orange fringed strip along the curved edge of the pink flap, on the right side.
2. Place the rights sides of the front and back pillow pieces together. Sew the 12-1/2" side seams. Turn right side out.
3. Sew a 1/4" seam along the bottom edge of the pillow cover.
4. Insert the pillow form and place the straight edge of the flap even with the top of the pillow. Sew a 1/4"

seam across the top edge of the pillow.

5. To make the red and orange flowers, gather one end of each ribbed ring. Pull the thread tight and secure. See Fig. 2.

6. To make the multi-colored flower bud, gather one edge of one ring and pull tight, like you did in Step 5.

7. To make the open flower, gather the ring 1/2" from one edge. Pull tight so the ring gathers to form a center in the flower. See Fig 3.

8. Sew the four flowers to the flap.

9. Gather each leaf down the middle. See Fig 4. Sew the leaves among the flowers, using the photo as a guide.

10. Hand sew the flap to the pillow front under the fringe. ✳

Fig. 1 - Cutting diagram.

Fig. 2 - Gathering a ribbed flower bud.

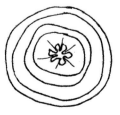

Fig. 3 - Open flower with center.

Fig. 4 - Leaf

Nine-Dot Pillow

Nine felted wool circles are arranged in three rows on the front of a wool pillow. The machine stitches that attach them form a grid.

SUPPLIES

Felted Wool:
- 2 pieces charcoal gray, each 14" square
- 9 circles, each 2-1/2" in diameter - assorted greens

Other Supplies:
- Pillow form, 14" square
- Black sewing thread
- Chalk

INSTRUCTIONS

1. On the pillow front, use chalk to make a grid for placing the circles. See Fig. 1.
2. Position the circles where the grid lines intersect. Stitch along the grid lines, attaching the circles. See Fig. 1.
3. With wrong sides together, sew a 1/2" seam along three sides of the pillow.
4. Insert the pillow form. Sew the fourth side of the pillow closed. ✳

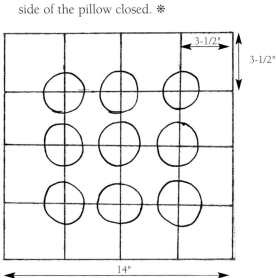

3-1/2"

3-1/2"

14"

Fig. 1 - Placement diagram.

Circles of Cuffs Pillow

Use the cuffs of your felted wool sweaters to create three-dimensional interest on a felted wool pillow.

SUPPLIES

Felted Wool:
- 2 pieces charcoal gray, each 16" square
- 9 sweater cuffs - Grays, browns, tans

Other Supplies:
- Pillow form, 16" square
- Black sewing thread
- Chalk
- Sewing machine

INSTRUCTIONS

1. Cut pieces of sweater cuffs 3" long. See Fig 1.
2. Fold cuffs in half, with the folds on top. See Fig 2.
3. With chalk, draw a 4" grid on the pillow front. See Fig 3.
4. Position a folded cuff at each intersection of the grid. Sew around each cuff to attach each one to the pillow front.
5. Place the pillow front on the pillow back with wrong sides together. Sew a 1/2" seam around three sides.
6. Insert the pillow form and sew the fourth side closed. ✳

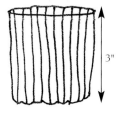

Fig. 1 - Cutting the cuffs.

Fold

Raw edges

Fig. 2 - Folding the cuffs.

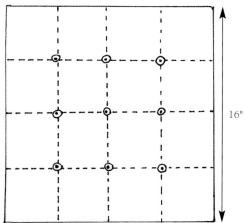

16"

Fig. 3 - Marking the 4" grid.

Loopy Stripes Pillow

Strips cut from a striped felted wool sweater are hand stitched to the front of a felted wool pillow, creating loopy, dimensional stripes. You could add the strips to a purchased pillow if you don't want to make one.

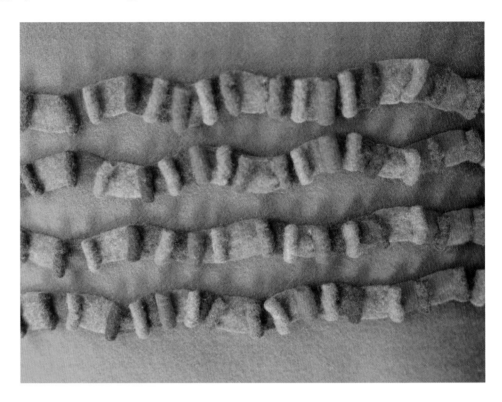

SUPPLIES

Felted Wool:
- 2 pieces green, each 16" square
- Multi-colored striped sweater

Other Supplies:
- Pillow form, 16" square
- Sewing thread to match strips
- Sewing machine

INSTRUCTIONS

1. Cut the sweater into strips 1" wide, with the stripes going the short way. See Fig 1.
2. Pink and sew the strips so that every other stripe makes a loop. See Fig. 2.
3. Position the looped strips across the pillow front, making four wavy lines from edge to edge. See photo for guide. *TIP: You may need to use more than one strip for each stripe.*
4. Sew the strips to the pillow.
5. Place the pillow front on the pillow back, right sides together. Sew around three sides. Turn.
6. Insert the pillow form. Sew the fourth side closed. ✸

1" wide

Fig. 1 - Cutting the strips.

Fig. 2 - Sewing the loop with every other stripe.

32 Squares Pillow

Thirty-two felted wool squares are pieced together using raw seam joins. This pillow has striped squares on one side and solid-color squares on the other, and is reversible for two different looks.

SUPPLIES

Felted Wool:
- 2 striped sweaters in different colors
- 1 solid-color sweater

Other Supplies:
- Pillow form, 14" square
- Sewing thread in matching colors
- Sewing machine

INSTRUCTIONS

Cut:
1. Cut eight 4" squares from one striped sweater.
2. Cut eight more 4" squares from the other striped sweater.
3. Cut sixteen 4" squares from the solid-colored sweater.

Assemble:
1. Arrange the striped squares in four rows with four squares to a row. Use the project photo and Fig. 1 as guides.
2. Sew the squares in each row together with 1/4" outside seams.
3. Sew the four rows together to make the pillow front.
4. Follow the same procedure, using the 16 solid-colored squares, to make the back.
5. With seams on the outside, sew the front and back of the pillow together. Leave one side partly open for inserting the pillow form.
6. Add the form and stitch the opening closed. ✳

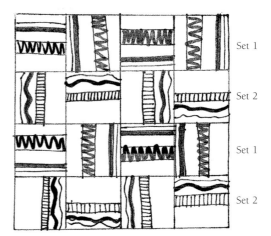

Fig. 1 - Placement diagram.

Set 1

Set 2

Set 1

Set 2

Crazy Quilt Trunk Top

The design of this padded pieced wool trunk top evokes the popular crazy quilts of the Victorian era. The embroidery on the pieces, except for the stitches on the seamlines, was on the sweaters before they were felted. I used only a trunk base, and made the top pieces from plywood and foam.

SUPPLIES

Felted Wool:
- 11 (or more) different types–embroidered, patterned, plaid, appliqued, etc.
- Solid brown, 33" x 19"

Other Supplies:
- Wool tapestry yarn - White, tan, dark red, gold, several greens
- Trunk base
- 3/4" plywood for trunk lid, 31" x 17" (or cut to the size of your trunk)
- 4 pieces 1 x 2 lumber - Two 12" long, two 6" long
- Nails and hammer
- Foam rubber, 3" x 31" x 17" (or cut to the size of your trunk)
- Spray glue (for foam rubber)
- Brown paint (to match brown felt)
- Paint brush
- Staple gun and strong staples

INSTRUCTIONS

1. Cut, arrange, and pin overlapping felted wool pieces, in a design of your choice. Pin as many pieces together as needed to make a piece 31" x 46".
2. Use one or many embroidery stitches to join the pieces of felted wool. See the Basic Techniques section for Hand Embroidery instructions. *Note:* It is not necessary to stitch around the outer edges of the piece.
3. Spray the top of the plywood with adhesive. Place the foam on top of the adhesive-coated surface. See Fig. 1.
4. Lay the pieced wool fabric over the foam, right side up. Turn everything over, wrap the pieced fabric around the foam and plywood, and staple the fabric to the bottom of the plywood, pulling the fabric tightly as you staple. See Fig. 2.
5. Place the brown felt over the bottom of the trunk top. Turn under the edges of the felt and, make sure the raw edges of the crazy quilt piece and the plywood are covered, staple the brown felt in place.
6. Paint the wooden trunk base and the slats with brown paint. Use as many coats as needed for solid coverage. Let dry completely.
7. Position the trunk lid on the trunk base and determine where to place the slats so they will sit inside the base and hold the lid in place. Nail the slats to the bottom of the trunk lid. See Fig. 3. ✳

Fig. 1 - Gluing the foam to the plywood.

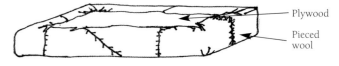

Fig. 2 - Wrapping the pieced wool around the trunk lid.

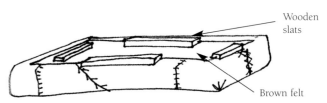

Fig. 3 - Placing the slats.

Purple Flower Stool

I used a stool with wrought iron legs and an upholstered top for this project, but you could use any type of stool with a removable top. Just cover the existing top or cut a new base from plywood, add foam rubber padding, and cover it. The top of my stool measures 15" x 15", and it is attached from the bottom with screws. Choose sturdy pieces of wool for the cover.

SUPPLIES

Felted Wool Pieces:
- Lavender
- Violet
- Lime green
- Burgundy

Other Supplies:
- Stool with detachable base
- Wool tapestry yarn - Lime green, light pink, medium pink, dark pink
- Water soluble stabilizer
- Staple gun and staples
- Sewing thread - Medium green, hot pink, violet
- Sewing machine

INSTRUCTIONS

Cut:
1. Cut a piece of lavender wool large enough to cover the top and sides and be pulled tautly around the bottom. (For my 15" x 15" stool, I cut a piece 19" x 19".)
2. Using the flower pattern provided, cut a flower from violet felt. Cut out the holes.
3. Cut another flower from burgundy felt, cutting it 1/4" larger all around than the pattern. Do **not** cut out the holes on this piece.
4. Cut four leaves from the green felt—two from each leaf pattern.

Sew:
1. Place the (smaller) violet flower on top of the (larger) burgundy flower. Pin to hold.
2. Place the flower layer on the center of the lavender square.
3. Position one leaf at each corner as shown, with the wide ends of the leaves under the burgundy flower. Pin the leaves in place on the lavender base square. Remove the flower layer.
4. Place a piece of stabilizer under the lavender square and sew around the leaves, attaching them to the lavender base. Use a satin stitch and hot pink sewing thread to machine stitch the edges and the veins of the leaves.
5. Using green thread and decorative machine stitches, sew along the center vein and along the edges of the leaves.
6. Finish the leaves with free motion straight stitches, going all over the leaves with green thread.
7. Place the flower back on top of the lavender base. Use violet sewing thread to satin stitch just inside the edge of the violet flower.
8. With one strand of lime green yarn, blanket stitch around each hole in the violet flower.
9. Fill each hole with seven to ten French knots, using three strands of yarn. Use medium pink yarn for one hole, dark pink for another, and light pink for a third. Fill the remaining holes with combinations of the three pinks. See the Basic Techniques section for French knot instructions.

Assemble:
1. Take the top off the stool.
2. Place the wool cover over the stool cushion. Pull the wool over and around the sides and secure it to the bottom of the base with staples.
3. Reinstall the top. ✳

Purple Flower Stool
Flower Pattern

Enlarge 200% for actual size

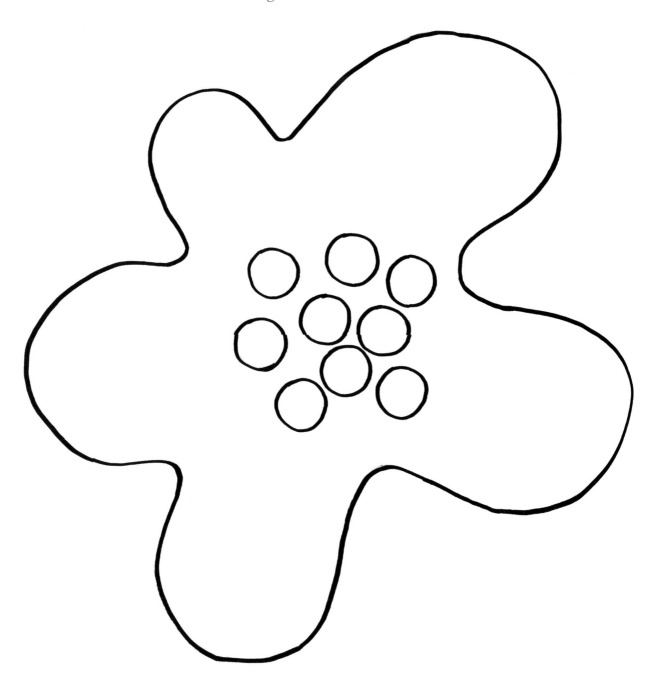

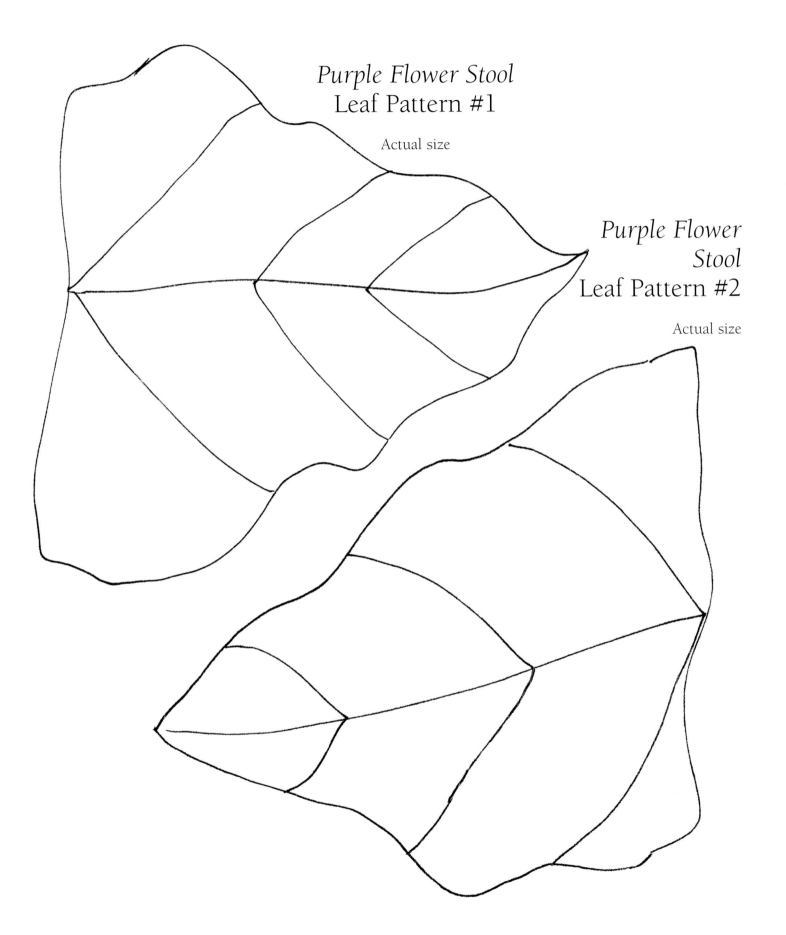

Purple Flower Stool
Leaf Pattern #1

Actual size

Purple Flower Stool
Leaf Pattern #2

Actual size

Reupholstered Round Ottoman

Felted wool makes a sturdy, colorful covering for the familiar round ottoman. Choose an ottoman with detachable legs for easy upholstery.

SUPPLIES
Felted Wool:
- Woven and knitted pieces of - Red, camel, charcoal, plaids

Other Supplies:
- Round ottoman with detachable legs, 18" diameter
- Staple gun and staples
- Black sewing thread
- Tracing paper and pencil
- Sewing machine
- *Optional:* 2" decorative button, black button thread, long needle

INSTRUCTIONS
Prepare:
1. Remove the legs from your ottoman. Remove the center tufting button, if your ottoman has one, from the top. Remove any fabric covering the bottom.
2. Trace the pattern provided *or* make a pattern for the top of your ottoman: Draw around the top on tracing paper, enlarge the shape 1" all around, and divide the circle into 12 equal sections. See Fig 1. Cut out one of those sections and use it as the pattern for all 12 pieces.

Cut & Sew:
1. Cut three pie shapes from each of four different felted wools–three plaid, three charcoal, three camel, three red.
2. Sew the pieces together to make a circle, using a 1/4" seam allowance with the seams on the outside.
3. Use the same colors of felted wool to make 3" wide strips that are 3" longer than the height of your stool (without the legs). If needed, piece some of the strips, sewing them together with 1/4" seams on the outside.
4. Sew all of the 3" strips together with 1/4" seams on the right side of the fabric. Piece enough of the strips to fit snugly around the ottoman. (The finished piece will be a tube shape.)
5. Place the pieced tube of strips around the side of the ottoman. Pin the top piece to the side piece.
6. With seams exposed, sew to join the top piece to the side piece, using a 1/4" seam allowance.

Upholster:
1. Place the cover over the ottoman. Use a staple gun to tightly secure the bottom edge of the cover to the bottom of the ottoman.
2. *If your ottoman had a center button,* replace it with a decorative button. Use a very, very long needle and a double length of button thread (at least three times as long as the height of the ottoman). Bring the threaded needle up through the bottom, then through the button shank, through the button shank again, and back down to the bottom of the stool. Pull the thread tight and secure to the bottom of the stool with staples and knots.
3. Cut a circle of felt 1" smaller than the bottom of the ottoman. Using a staple gun, attach the felt circle to the bottom, covering all raw edges.
4. Re-attach the legs. ✳

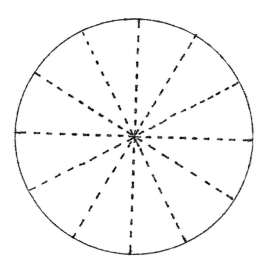

Fig. 1 - Top diagram.

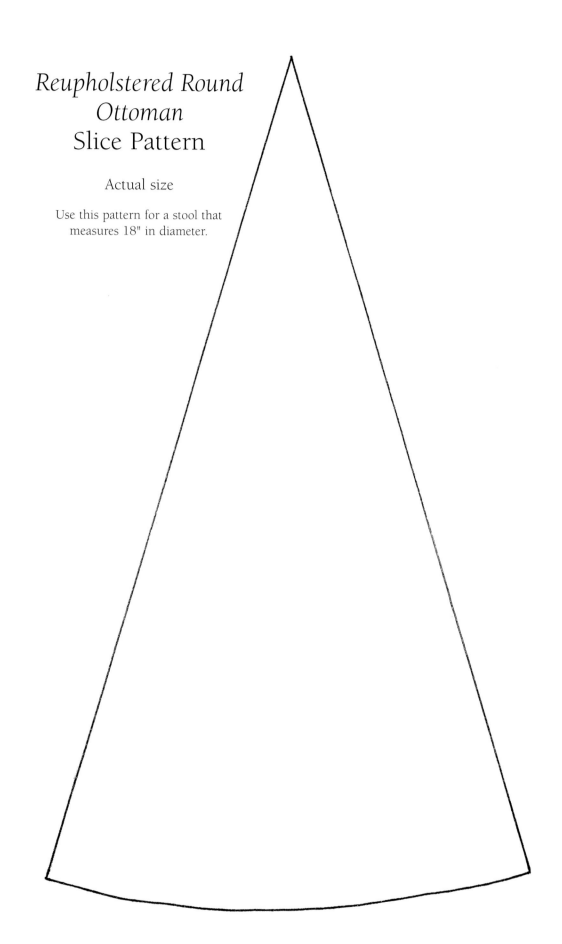

Reupholstered Round Ottoman Slice Pattern

Actual size

Use this pattern for a stool that measures 18" in diameter.

Appliqued Chair Cover Pictured on page 47.
Alphabet Patterns
Enlarge 350%.

Appliqued Chair Cover

Felted wool can be used to make comfortable, decorative covers for chair backs that can be personalized with monograms. Here are two options.

Pictured on the opposite page.

SUPPLIES
Felted Wool:
- Blacks and grays (for cover)
- Green (for monogram)
- Black (for monogram)
- Multi-colored striped

Other Supplies:
- Black sewing thread
- Measuring tape
- Tracing paper
- Sewing machine

INSTRUCTIONS

1. Measure the width of the top of the chair back and add 2". Compare this measurement with the pattern provided. Adjust the width of the pattern to fit your chair. Trace and enlarge the pattern.
2. Choose the monogram and enlarge as needed. Trace pattern and cut out.
3. Sew pieces of felted wool together to make a big enough piece for chair cover pattern. Place pattern on pieced wool and cut out the chair cover piece.
4. Place monogram initial pattern on black wool and cut out.
5. From green wool, cut the same monogram initial, but make the green wool initial 1/4" larger on all edges than the black letter.
6. Center the black letter on the green letter. Pin the two stacked letters at the center of the triangular flap, placing the bottom of the letter 5" above the point of the flap. See Fig. 1.
7. Attach the letter to the flap using a straight stitch. Using the straight stitch, sew wavy designs all over the surface of the letter.
8. Cut seventeen 1" felted wool squares from a striped sweater.
9. Place one 1" square 3/4" up from the center bottom point on the back of the cover. Place eight squares on each side of the center one. Stitch the squares from corner to corner as shown in the photo.
10. To close the cover, match the two straight ends of the cover. Overlap these ends and stitch the two ends together with an overlock stitch. This seam will be at the center back of the chair cover.
11. To use, slide the open straight end of the cover down over the chair back with the v-point hanging down at back of chair. ✳

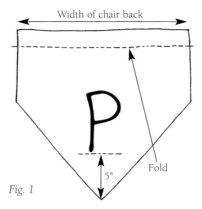

Fig. 1

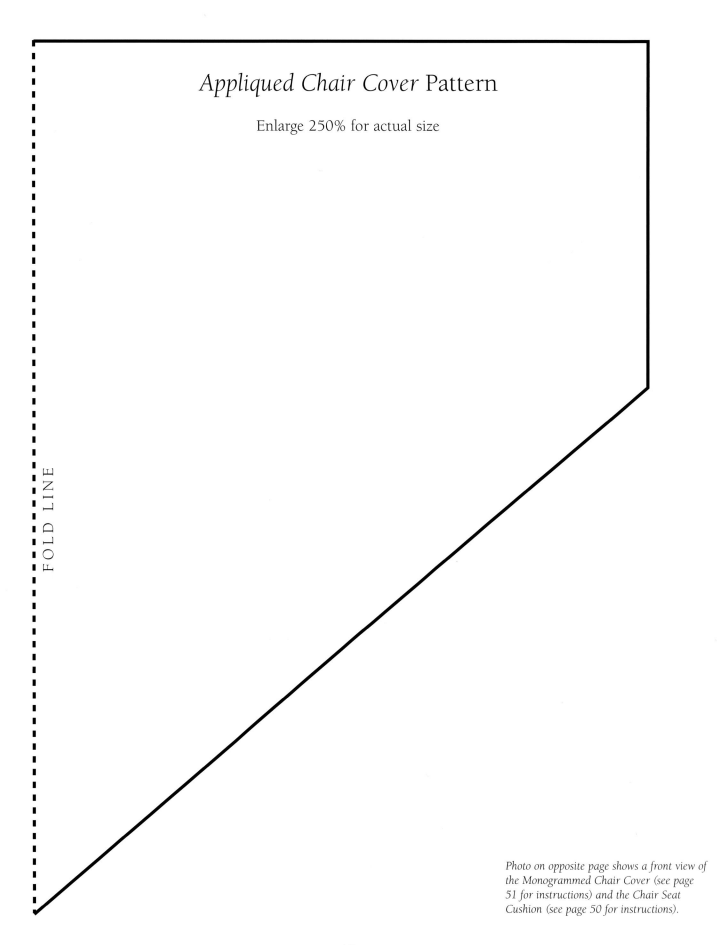

Appliqued Chair Cover Pattern

Enlarge 250% for actual size

FOLD LINE

Photo on opposite page shows a front view of the Monogrammed Chair Cover (see page 51 for instructions) and the Chair Seat Cushion (see page 50 for instructions).

Chair Seat Cushion

A seat cushion makes a wooden chair more comfortable and protects the seat on an upholstered one.

SUPPLIES

Felted Wool:
• Pieces in black and shades of gray

Other Supplies:
• 2" thick foam pad (larger than the chair seat)
• 1-1/2 yds. black velvet ribbon, 7/8" wide
• Black sewing thread
• Water soluble stabilizer
• Tape measure
• Sewing machine

INSTRUCTIONS

1. Measure the chair seat and cut the foam in the shape of the seat.
2. Piece the felted wool to make two pieces, each 1" wider and 1" longer than the shape of the foam. Use a closed overlock stitch and stabilizer to join the pieces.
3. With wrong sides together, stitch a 1/2" seam around the two sides and front of the cushion cover.
4. Insert the foam and sew the back seam closed.
5. Cut the velvet ribbon into two pieces, each 27" (3/4 yd.) long. Sew the center of each ribbon piece to one back corner of the cushion. Tie the ribbon in bows to hold the seat cushion to the back of the chair. ✳

Monogrammed Chair Cover

For this cover I sent my wool felted cover to a monogram shop to have it professionally monogrammed.

SUPPLIES
- Black
- Gray

Other Supplies:
- Black sewing thread
- Tape measure
- Sewing machine

INSTRUCTIONS

1. Cut black and gray felted wool into strips of varying widths approximately 11" long.
2. Measure the width of your chair back. From the wool pieces, create two pieces of fabric, each 10" deep and the width of the chair back plus 2".
3. Sew a monogram on one of the fabric pieces. (You can sew the monogram yourself or do what I did–take it to a professional.)
3. With right sides out, pin and then sew across the top and along the two sides, using a 1" seam allowance. ✳

Flower Cuts Rug

Simple flower appliques are created from colorful cutouts of felted wool and mounted on felted wool circles that are arranged on a black rectangle. Simple straight stitching, done on a sewing machine with black thread, holds everything together. It's a good idea to put a liner pad under this rug to keep it from sliding.

Finished size: 21" x 26"

SUPPLIES

Felted Wool:
- 2 pieces of black, each 21" x 26"
- Pieces of medium green, purple, violet, red, blue, light green, lavender, yellow, orange, pink, dark green

Other Supplies:
- Several spools of black sewing thread
- Sewing machine
- Tracing paper and pencil

INSTRUCTIONS

1. Following the arrangement in Fig. 1, the Circle Color Guide, cut a total of twenty 4-1/2" circles in the colors indicated.
2. Using the patterns provided and Fig. 2, the Design Color Guide, cut out the pieces for the various flower designs.
3. Assemble and sew the pieces of the various flower designs to the circles.

4. Stack the two 21" x 26" pieces of black felt on top of each other.
5. Arrange the circles, with designs attached, as indicated in Fig. 3, the Design Position Guide. Hand baste each in place with black thread.
6. To secure the circles to the black felt rectangles, free motion straight stitch all over the rug. **Note:** This entails a lot of sewing, and you'll use more than one spool of thread. All the pieces should be securely attached to the rug, with no parts sticking up or loose. (You don't want someone to catch a toe and trip, causing a fall.) ✳

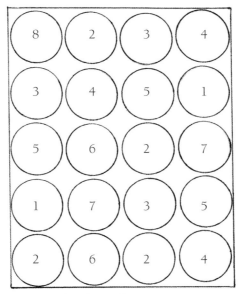

Fig. 1 - Circle Color Guide

1 - Medium green
2 - Purple
3 - Violet
4 - Red
5 - Blue
6 - Light green
7 - Lavender
8 - Dark green

continued on page 54

52

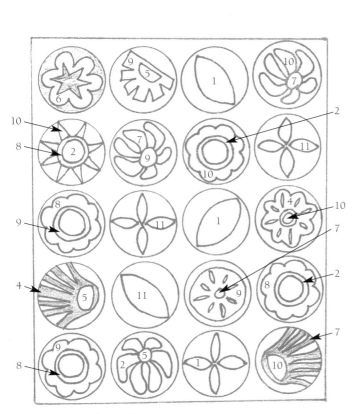

Fig. 2 - Design Color Guide

1 - Medium green   7 - Lavender
2 - Purple   8 - Yellow
3 - Violet   9 - Orange
4 - Red   10 - Pink
5 - Blue   11 - Dark green
6 - Light green

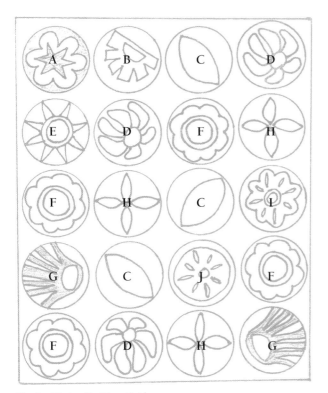

Fig. 3 - Design Position Guide

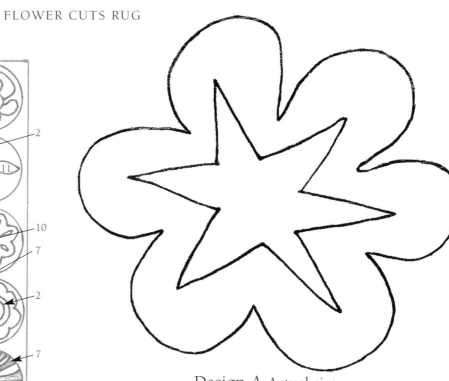

Design A Actual size
The base color shows through the center cutout.

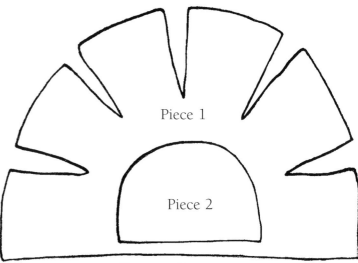

Piece 1

Piece 2

Design B Actual size

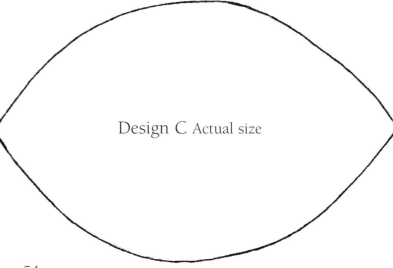

Design C Actual size

54

Piece 1

Piece 1

Piece 2

Design F
Actual size
Cut out the centers of both pieces. Place Piece 1 over Piece 2.

Piece 2

Design D
Actual size

Design E
Actual size

Piece 2

Piece 1

Piece 3

Design H
Actual size

Cut 4

Design G Actual size

Piece 2

Cut along the lines on Piece 2 and spread them on the circle. Place Piece 1 on the solid part of Piece 2.

Piece 1

Design I
Actual size
Cut out the centers of both pieces and the petal rays on Piece 1. Piece 2 fits over the center of Piece 1.

Piece 2

Piece 1

Design J
Actual size
Piece 2 fits under the hole in the center of Piece 1.

Piece 2

Piece 1

Appliqued Placemat
Patterns for
Appliques
Instructions are on page 58

Enlarge 200% for actual size

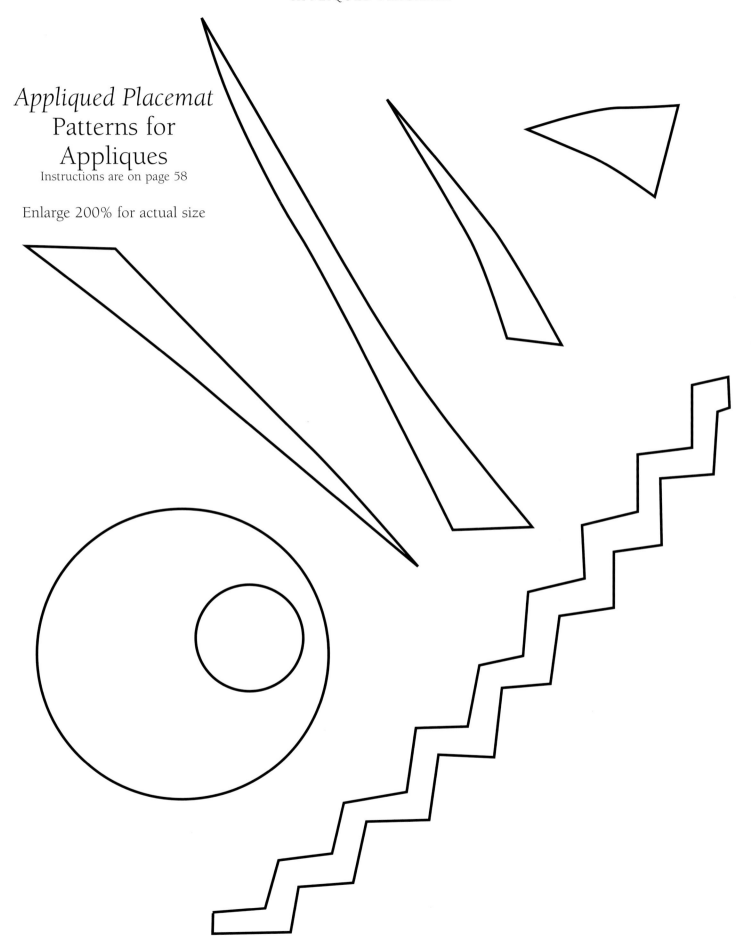

Appliqued Placemat

Pattern on page 57.

This placemat, pieced and appliqued from a range of neutral colors, has a decidedly modern look. For a completely different effect, try using a range of bright colors instead of black and grays.

Finished size: 19" x 13"

SUPPLIES

Felted Wool:
• A range of neutrals–Light gray, medium gray, dark gray, black

Other Supplies:
• Water soluble stabilizer
• Black sewing thread
• Sewing machine

INSTRUCTIONS

1. Using Fig. 1 as a guide, cut the pieces for the background of the placemat. The strips should be 13" long. Cut the widths as shown in Fig. 1, cutting unevenly. Cut pieces slightly wider than shown to allow for overlap for joining pieces.
2. Position the pieces, overlapping the edges. With stabilizer under the layers, stitch the pieces together with an overcast stitch. Trim to even the edges.
3. Using the patterns, cut the applique pieces. Use the photo as a guide for color choice.
4. Position the appliques as shown in photo. Machine sew with a straight stitch.
5. Using the sewing machine, straight stitch in free motion all over the placemat, using black thread. ✳

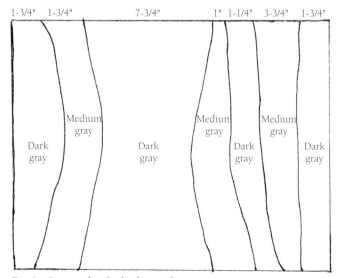

Fig. 1 - Piecing plan for background.

Coiled Oval Rug

Coiled thin strips of felted wool make a colorful and comfortable rug. Vary the colors and combinations to coordinate with your decor, or design your rug to accommodate the sweaters you want to use. Roll all the coils and wraps tightly so the rug will be sturdy.

Finished Size: 22" x 19"

SUPPLIES

Felted Wool:
• Pullover sweaters - Red, light blue, red print, navy blue, light and dark blue print, charcoal

Other Supplies:
• Black sewing thread
• Sewing needle

Fig. 1 - Construction diagram.

INSTRUCTIONS

1. Cut all the felted wool into strips 1/2" wide and as long as possible. See the Basic Techniques section for instructions on cutting a continuous strip from a sweater.
2. See the legend that accompanies Fig. 1 to see how long to cut the strips to make coils, the color to cut them from, and how to connect the different pieces together. Start with the center coil. As you roll the coil, sew it through the middle of the strip, using a double thread and a sewing needle, so the thread doesn't show.
3. Continue with the rest of the coils, connecting them as indicated in Fig. 1. Keep the coils as tight and compact as possible. When joining coils, stitch several layers of one to several layers of the other. Sew through the middles of the strips so no stitches show. *Option:* Work on the back side to secure the coils and sections of the rug. The stitches don't need to be hidden if they are kept on the back side of the rug, but if you do, the rug won't be reversible. Add more coils and wraps if you want a larger rug. ✳

Legend

A - Red coil from a 9" strip, tight coil.

B - Red print coil from 30" strip, tight coil.

C - Red print coil from 15" strip, tight coil.

D - Red strip, wrapped tightly in one layer around A, B, and C coils.

E - Light blue strips and coils. Use coils of different sizes to fill in the larger spaces. Add strips to complete the wrap, evening out the oval shape.

F - Dark blue strips, wrapped four times around the perimeter, keeping the oval shape.

G - Double coil, made with a 30" strip of light and dark blue print and a red 23" strip. Place the two strips together, lining up the ends, with the red strip on the inside. Roll and sew the coil together. (You will end up with more blue, but just keep coiling and secure the end.) Make 12. Flatten them up against the dark blue border strips (F) and sew. Connect the sides of the coils to each other.

H - Red coil from 10" strip. Make 12. Shape the coils to fit between the previous coils (G) and round out the oval shape.

I - Charcoal strips, wrapped three times around the oval shape.

J - Zig-zag border, 2" wide, made of red strips. Fold a long red strip back and forth, making fan folds 2" wide. Fold and sew strips together to form a border all around the oval. Sew the inner edge of each loop on the border to the charcoal strips (I).

K - Charcoal strips, wrapped five times. Complete the rug with five wraps of charcoal strips. Sew the first wrap of charcoal strips to the outer edge of each loop in the red fan-fold border (J). Sew the remaining wraps as you go.

Scalloped Edge Rug

A simple rug of pieced strips has a border of blanket-stitched circles, placed to create a scalloped edge. Machine overlock stitching is used for the strips; the blanket stitching is done with wool tapestry yarn.

Finished size: 30" x 24"

SUPPLIES
Felted Wool:
• Sweaters with a variety of patterned designs in brown, blue, off-white, black and blue
• Solid black

Other Supplies:
• Wool tapestry yarn - Rust, tan
• Water soluble stabilizer
• Black sewing thread
• Sewing machine

INSTRUCTIONS
Piece the Rug:
1. Cut strips of felted wool 28" long and any width from 2" to 5".
2. Lay all the pieces side by side, with edges overlapping approximately 3/4", to make a piece 22" wide.
3. With stabilizer under the overlaps, use an overlock machine stitch to sew the pieces together.
4. Trim the rug to 26" x 21-1/2". (Sewing, then trimming allows you to even the edges and control the size.)

Add the Border:
1. Using the patterns provided, cut thirty-six 2-1/2" black circles and thirty-six 1-1/2" patterned circles.

2. Place a patterned circle at the center of each black circle. Blanket stitch the patterned circle to the black circle with two strands of tan yarn.
3. Blanket stitch around each black circle with two strands of rust yarn.
4. Pin the circles around the outer edge of the rug as shown in the photo, with half of each circle under the edge of the rug.
5. Hand sew the circles to the front edges of the rug.
6. Hand sew the circles to the back of the rug. ✱

Tan yarn   Rust yarn

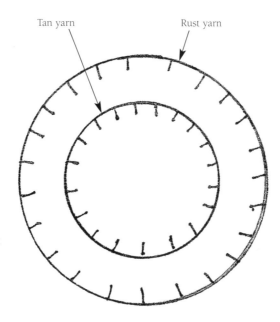

Pattern
Actual size

Cut 36 of each circle.

Sweet Dreams Baby Blanket

This blanket is baby safe because it has no removable parts. Pick very soft wools for comfort.

Finished size: 40" x 51" (approx.)

SUPPLIES

Felted Wool:

- Scraps of various pastel shades (See the patterns for suggested colors.)
- 48 squares in pastel colors, each 6"
- Ribbing, 3" wide, from the bottoms of seven or more felted sweaters (for the ruffle, avoid using heavy or sturdy sweaters)

Other Supplies:

- Yellow fleece *or* soft wool, 40" x 50" (for backing)
- White sewing thread
- Wool yarn - Green, light orange, black, yellow, orange, pink, white, dark brown, brown, blue, light blue, red, golden yellow (See the Stitching Guides for suggested colors for each design.)
- Cord *or* heavy-duty thread (for gathering the ruffle)
- Sewing machine

INSTRUCTIONS

The patterns appear on pages 68 and 69.

1. Using the patterns provided, from the pastel wool scraps cut out the pieces of the 12 applique designs. (Colors and cutting instructions appear with the patterns.)
2. Follow the instructions in the Stitching Guides to assemble the appliques and stitch them to 12 of the 48 pastel squares. Use the photo as a guide for color choices.
3. Using the photo on page 63 as a guide, arrange the 48 squares to make the blanket. With wrong sides facing, sew all of the squares together, using 1/4" seams.
4. Sew all the ribbing strips together, end to end.
5. Sew a gathering cord along one long side of the pieced ribbing strips. Lightly gather the edge to form a ruffle.
6. Pin the gathered edge of the ruffle along the underside of the edges of the blanket, evenly spacing the gathers and leaving the ruffle to the outside. Place the pins close together.
7. Sew the ruffle to the blanket with a 1/4" seam allowance. (Closely spacing the pins will ensure that the presser foot does not push the ruffle flat.)
8. Place the backing on the back of the blanket. Pin. Sew the backing to the blanket, stitching along the same line used to sew the ruffle. Trim the backing to 1/4" from the stitching line. ✳

Stitching Guides for Designs

See the Basic Techniques sections for Hand Embroidery instructions.

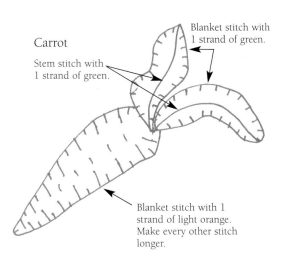

Carrot

Stem stitch with 1 strand of green.

Blanket stitch with 1 strand of green.

Blanket stitch with 1 strand of light orange. Make every other stitch longer.

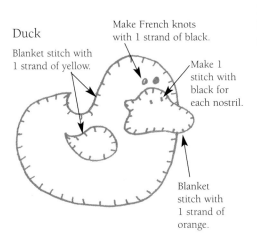

Duck

Blanket stitch with 1 strand of yellow.

Make French knots with 1 strand of black.

Make 1 stitch with black for each nostril.

Blanket stitch with 1 strand of orange.

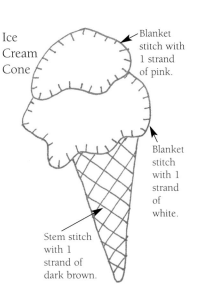

Ice Cream Cone

Blanket stitch with 1 strand of pink.

Blanket stitch with 1 strand of white.

Stem stitch with 1 strand of dark brown.

Continued on page 66

Stitching Guides for Designs, continued.

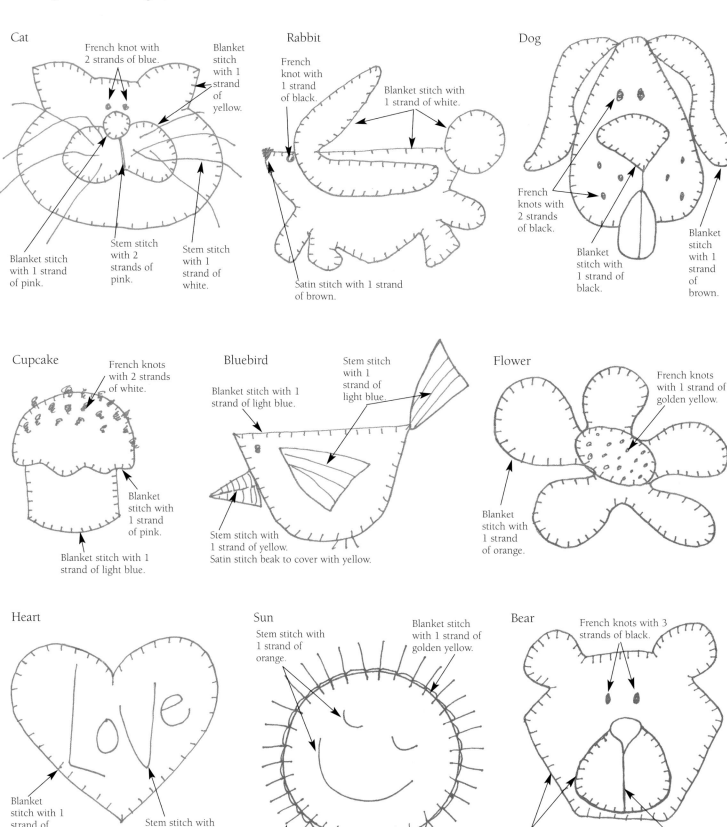

Cat

French knot with 2 strands of blue.

Blanket stitch with 1 strand of yellow.

Blanket stitch with 1 strand of pink.

Stem stitch with 2 strands of pink.

Stem stitch with 1 strand of white.

Rabbit

French knot with 1 strand of black.

Blanket stitch with 1 strand of white.

Satin stitch with 1 strand of brown.

Dog

French knots with 2 strands of black.

Blanket stitch with 1 strand of black.

Blanket stitch with 1 strand of brown.

Cupcake

French knots with 2 strands of white.

Blanket stitch with 1 strand of pink.

Blanket stitch with 1 strand of light blue.

Bluebird

Blanket stitch with 1 strand of light blue.

Stem stitch with 1 strand of light blue.

Stem stitch with 1 strand of yellow. Satin stitch beak to cover with yellow.

Flower

French knots with 1 strand of golden yellow.

Blanket stitch with 1 strand of orange.

Heart

Blanket stitch with 1 strand of orange.

Stem stitch with 1 strand of red.

Sun

Stem stitch with 1 strand of orange.

Blanket stitch with 1 strand of golden yellow.

Stem stitch with 1 strand of golden yellow.

Bear

French knots with 3 strands of black.

Blanket stitch with 1 strand of brown.

Stem stitch with 2 strands of black

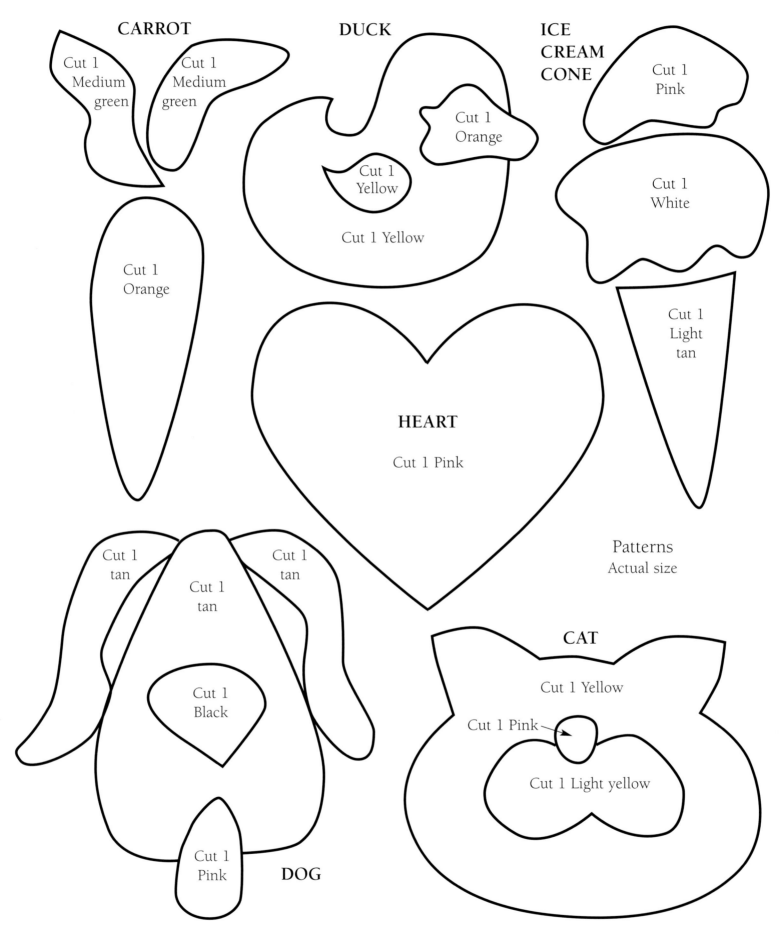

CARROT

Cut 1 Medium green

Cut 1 Medium green

Cut 1 Orange

DUCK

Cut 1 Orange

Cut 1 Yellow

Cut 1 Yellow

ICE CREAM CONE

Cut 1 Pink

Cut 1 White

Cut 1 Light tan

HEART

Cut 1 Pink

Patterns
Actual size

Cut 1 tan

Cut 1 tan

Cut 1 tan

Cut 1 Black

Cut 1 Pink

DOG

CAT

Cut 1 Yellow

Cut 1 Pink

Cut 1 Light yellow

SUN

Cut 1
Yellow

FLOWER

Cut 1
Pink

Cut 1
Yellow

CUPCAKE

Cut 1
Pink

Cut 1
Turquoise

BLUEBIRD

Cut 1
Yellow

Cut 1
Medium blue

Cut 1
Medium
blue

Cut 1
Medium blue

RABBIT

Cut 1
White

Cut 1 White

Cut 1 White

BEAR

Cut 1 tan

Cut 1 Black

Cut 1
Light
tan

Heart Hot Water Bottle Cover

Express your heartfelt love and concern with this cozy hot water bottle cover. Choose very soft wools for hot water bottle covers.

SUPPLIES

Felted Wool:
- Gray (for the cover)
- Scrap of red (for the heart)

Other Supplies:
- 1 yd. black grosgrain ribbon, 7/8" wide
- Hot water bottle
- Wool tapestry yarn - Black, dark red
- Black sewing thread
- *Optional:* Sewing machine

INSTRUCTIONS

1. Using the pattern provided, cut a front and back bottle cover from gray wool. TIP: Place the open end of the cover on the bottom of the sweater, using the ribbing for the top of the cover. Cut the marked slits for the ribbon on both pieces.
2. Using the pattern provided, cut the heart from red wool.
3. Pin the heart to the front of the bottle cover. Use two strands of dark red yarn to sew it in place with straight hand stitches.
4. With wrong sides together, sew a 3/8" seam around the sides and bottom of the cover.
5. Using three strands of black yarn, blanket stitch around the sides and bottom.
6. Thread the ribbon through the holes around the neck of the bottle cover, starting and stopping on the front.
7. Insert the water bottle. Tie the ribbon in a bow. ✳

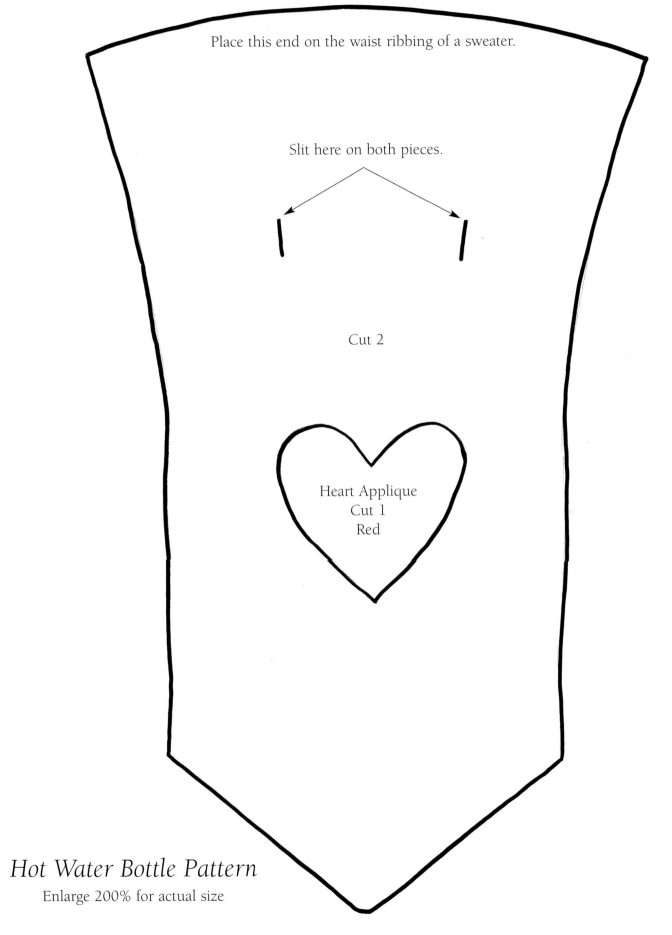

Place this end on the waist ribbing of a sweater.

Slit here on both pieces.

Cut 2

Heart Applique
Cut 1
Red

Hot Water Bottle Pattern
Enlarge 200% for actual size

Lamb Hot Water Bottle Cover

This hot water bottle cover looks cozy, won't slip around, and protects the skin from too much heat. Choose very soft wools for hot water bottle covers.

SUPPLIES

Felted Wool:
- Red
- Off-white sweater sleeve
- Small amounts of off-white, black

Other Supplies:
- 1 yd. green grosgrain ribbon with blue dots, 7/8" wide
- Hot water bottle
- Wool tapestry yarn - Off-white, medium blue
- Heavy white thread
- Black sewing thread
- *Optional:* Sewing machine

INSTRUCTIONS

1. Using the pattern provided, cut a front and back bottle cover from red wool. Cut the marked slits for the ribbon in both pieces.
2. Using the patterns provided, cut one ear and one lamb's body from off-white wool. Cut the head and four 3/8" x 2" strips for legs from black wool.
3. Cut a continuous strip 1/2" wide from off-white wool. See the Basic Techniques section for instructions on cutting a continuous strip. TIP: Use one sleeve with the cuff cut off for this.
4. Using heavy white thread, gather the off-white strip down the middle. See Fig 1.
5. Sew the gathered strip to the lamb's body, covering it completely. Extend the strip at top of the lamb's back 1-1/8" to make the tail.
6. Pin the lamb's body to the bottle cover front. Place the head and legs in position.
7. With black sewing thread, hand sew the legs and head to the cover, using a blanket stitch. With the white thread, hand sew the body and tail to the bottle cover. Blanket stitch the ear to the head with white thread.
8. To make the lamb's eye, first use three strands of off-white yarn to sew three overlapping stitches, each 1/8" long, going from side to side. See Fig 2.
9. Using one strand of blue yarn, stitch up and down twice over the center of the white stitches, forming the eyeball. See Fig. 3.
10. With right sides together, sew the sides and bottom of the two pieces of the bottle cover together. Turn to right side.
11. Thread the ribbon through the holes around the neck of the bottle cover, starting and stopping on the front.
12. Insert the water bottle. Pull the ribbon snugly and tie in a bow. ✳

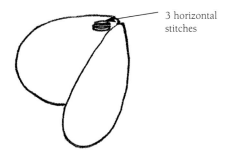

Fig. 1 - Gathering the off-white strip.

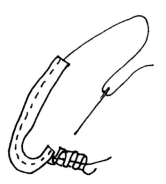

3 horizontal stitches

Fig. 2 - Stitching the lamb's eye with off-white yarn.

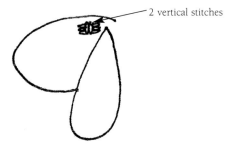

2 vertical stitches

Fig. 3 - Stitching the lamb's eyeball with blue yarn.

Lamb Patterns

Actual size

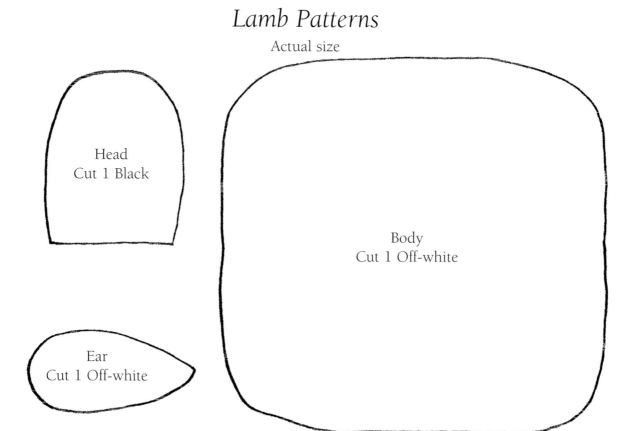

Head
Cut 1 Black

Ear
Cut 1 Off-white

Body
Cut 1 Off-white

Hot Water Bottle Pattern Enlarge 200% for actual size

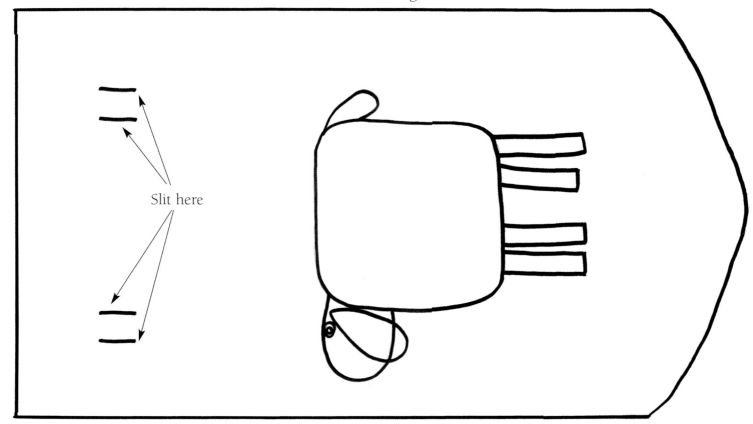

Slit here

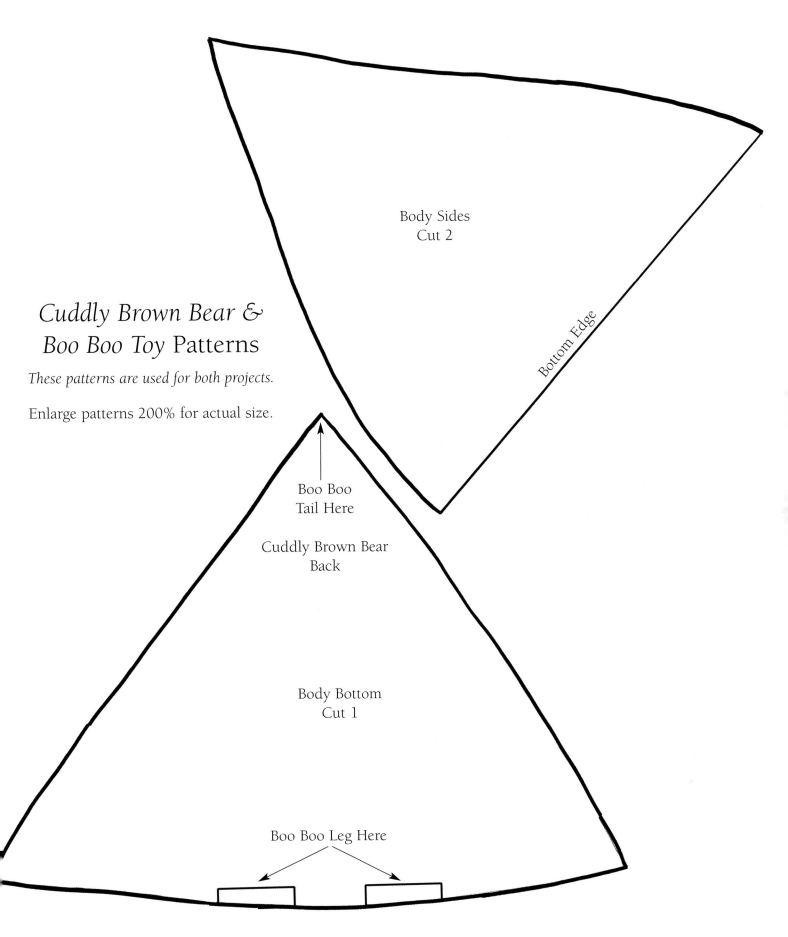

Body Sides
Cut 2

Bottom Edge

Cuddly Brown Bear & Boo Boo Toy Patterns

These patterns are used for both projects.

Enlarge patterns 200% for actual size.

Boo Boo
Tail Here

Cuddly Brown Bear
Back

Body Bottom
Cut 1

Boo Boo Leg Here

Cuddly Brown Bear

Brown felted wool makes a wonderful bear. For safety with infants, instead of using buttons for eyes and belly button, sew on rounds of wool fabric, or embroidered eyes and belly button.

SUPPLIES

Felted Wool:
- Browns of different shades
- Scraps of red, white

Other Supplies:
- Wool tapestry yarn - White
- 2 blue buttons, 3/4"
- 1 brown button, 5/8"
- 2 black buttons, 3/8"
- Polyester stuffing
- Water soluble stabilizer
- Black sewing thread
- Sewing machine
- Strong thread and sewing needle
- Tracing paper and pencil

INSTRUCTIONS

Cut:
1. Using the patterns provided on pages 75 and 78, cut from darker brown wool: two hands, two feet, one bottom, and two heads.
2. From medium brown wool, cut two arms, each 8" x 4-1/2", and two legs, each 5" x 11".
3. Using the patterns provided, cut from medium brown wool: one snout, two sides, and one front.
4. Using the pattern, cut one nose from red wool.
5. Using the pattern, cut 2 eyes from white wool.

Sew the Body:
All seams are 1/4" and on the outside.
1. Fold each arm piece in half to form pieces 4" x 4-1/2". Sew each arm seam. See Fig. 1.

2. Sew one open end of each arm tube to a round hand piece. See Fig. 2.
3. Fold each leg in half to form pieces 5" x 6-1/2". Sew the leg seams.
4. Sew one open end of each leg tube to the round foot piece.
5. Sew the brown belly button to center of body, using white yarn.
6. Lightly stuff the arms and legs. Pinch the open ends of the arms and legs flat, with the seams of each to the bottom side, and pin them to the front side of the bear as indicated on the pattern. See Fig. 3.
7. Sew the two body sides to the body front. Sew the two sides together to form the back seam, leaving an opening at the top point of the body for stuffing.
8. Sew the bottom of the body onto the body front and sides.
9. Stuff the body softly. Stitch the opening shut.

Sew the Head:
1. Place the snout and white eyes on the bear face. With stabilizer under the bear face, sew the snout and eyes to the face, using a zig-zag stitch.
2. Sew the nose onto the face, overlapping the snout.
3. Sew button eyes (black buttons on top of blue buttons) on the white eyes.
4. Place the head front and back with wrong sides together and sew around the entire head, leaving a small opening at the bottom for stuffing. Also sew across the bottoms of the ears.
5. Lightly stuff the head. Sew the opening closed.
6. Using a needle and strong thread, come up from the back at the base of the nose, and come back down below the snout. Pull tightly, causing the snout to pucker. Secure the thread.
7. Place the head at the top of the front of the body. Sew the head to the body. See Fig. 4. ✳

Fig. 1 - Stitching the arm seam.

Fig. 2 - Adding the hand at one end of the arm.

Fig. 3 - Joining the arms and legs to the body front.

Fig. 4 - Adding the head to the body.

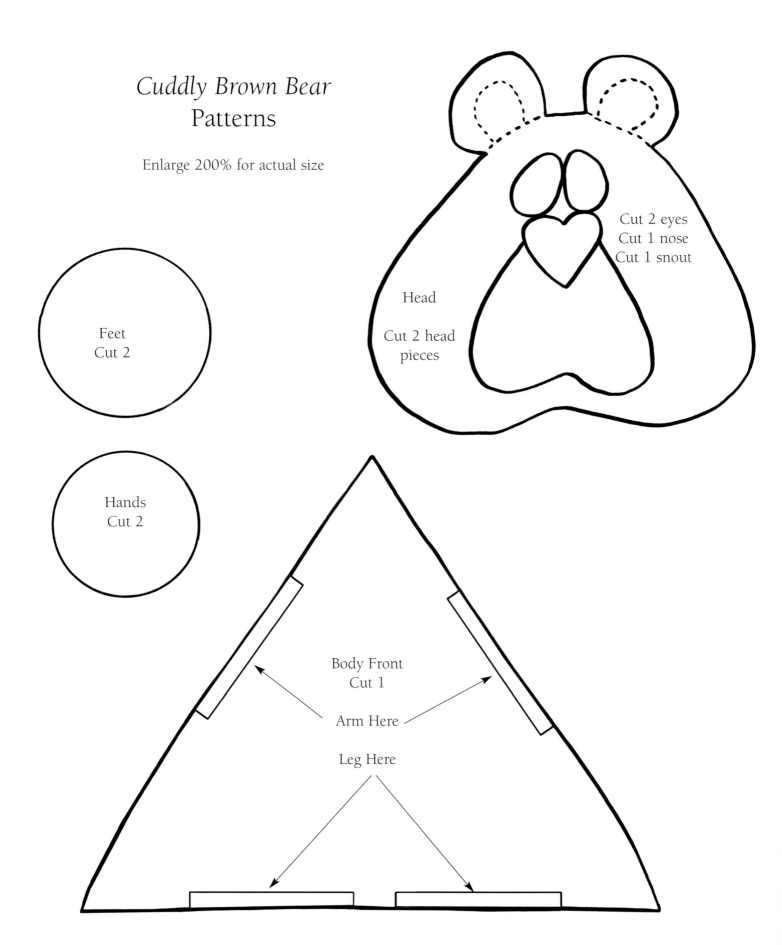

Cuddly Brown Bear
Patterns

Enlarge 200% for actual size

Feet
Cut 2

Hands
Cut 2

Cut 2 eyes
Cut 1 nose
Cut 1 snout

Head

Cut 2 head
pieces

Body Front
Cut 1

Arm Here

Leg Here

Boo Boo Toy Patterns

Enlarge patterns 200% for actual size.

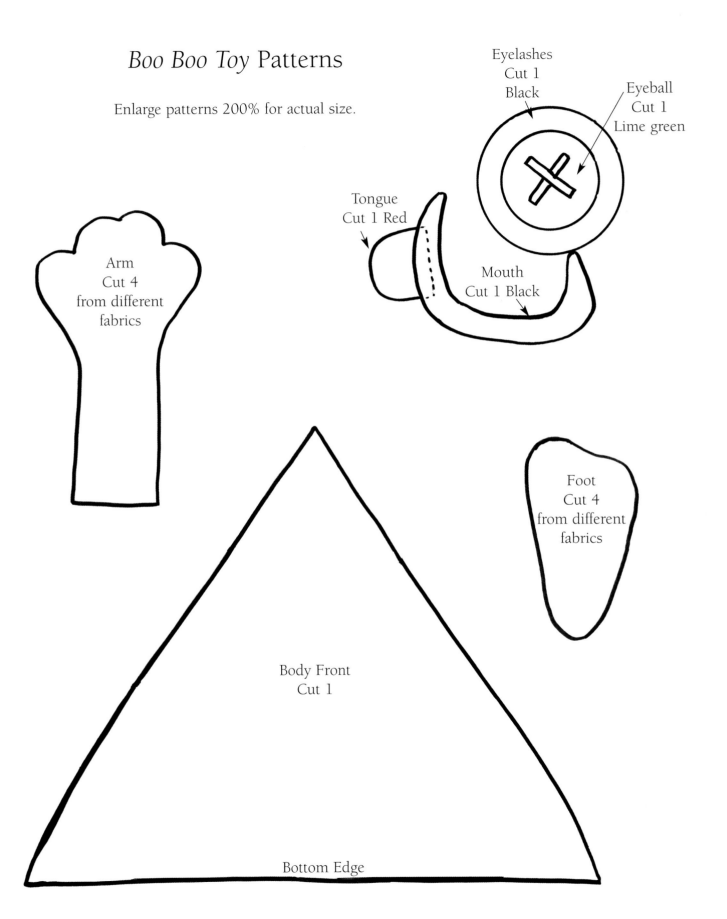

Eyelashes
Cut 1
Black

Eyeball
Cut 1
Lime green

Tongue
Cut 1 Red

Mouth
Cut 1 Black

Arm
Cut 4
from different
fabrics

Foot
Cut 4
from different
fabrics

Body Front
Cut 1

Bottom Edge

Boo Boo Toy

This grinning stuffed toy is bound to elicit smiles. Use a variety of colors and patterns for best results.

SUPPLIES

Felted Wool:
- Assorted unmatched pieces
- Scraps of black, lime green

Other Supplies:
- Polyester stuffing
- Water soluble stabilizer (for front piece)
- Black sewing thread
- Tracing paper and pencil
- Sewing machine

INSTRUCTIONS

Cut:

1. Using the patterns provided on pages 75 and 79, with no matching parts touching, cut from felted wool: one front, two sides, one bottom, four feet, and four arms. Plan the arrangement so no pieces cut from the same color or pattern will touch.
2. From different pieces of felted wool, cut two legs, each 12" x 3".
3. Cut the face details from these colors:
   Mouth and eyelashes - Black
   Tongue - Red
   Eyeball - Lime green
4. For hair, cut four strips, each 1/2" x 14", from four different wools.

Sew:

All seams are on the outside and 1/4". Use black thread for all stitching.

1. Place stabilizer on the back of the front piece. Sew the mouth, with the tongue placed just underneath it, on one side. Use a zig-zag stitch around the mouth, but don't sew the bottom part of the tongue–leave it loose.
2. Center the green eye on top of the black eyelashes piece. Zig-zag around the edge of the green eye. Satin stitch the X on the center of the green eye.
3. Cut the black eyelashes piece every 1/4" from the edge to the green eye.
4. Place the pairs of arm pieces with wrong sides together. Sew around them.
5. With wrong sides together, fold the leg pieces lengthwise. Sew the side seam.
6. With wrong sides together, sew around both feet.
7. Open one end of one leg, position on the top of one foot, and sew in place. See Fig. 1. Repeat with the other leg and foot.
8. Sew the arms and legs to the front.
9. Sew the two body sides to the body front. Sew the two sides together to form the back seam, leaving an opening at the top for the stuffing and hair pieces.
10. Sew the bottom on the toy.
11. Stuff the body through the hole.
12. Fold the hair strips in half and stitch them together at the centers. (Fig. 2) Push the centers of the pieces into the top of the head and sew closed. See Fig. 3. ✳

Fig. 1 - Sewing the leg to the foot.

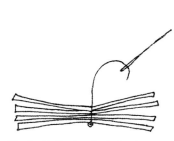

Fig. 2 - Gathering the hair pieces at the centers.

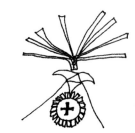

Fig. 3 - Inserting the hair in the top of the head.

Penguin Pal

I used a combination of woven and knitted felted wool to make this project. You can vary the penguin's expression by changing the position of the eyeballs.

SUPPLIES
Felted Wool:
- Woven or knitted- Black, white, orange
- Scraps of green

Other Supplies:
- 10 oz. polyester stuffing
- Polyester batting, 10" square
- Sewing thread - Black, white, orange, green
- Tracing paper and pencil
- Sewing machine

INSTRUCTIONS
Cut:
1. Using the patterns provided on pages 84 and 85, cut from black wool: two sides, four wings, one back, and two eyes.
2. Using the patterns provided, cut from white wool: one front belly and two eyeballs.
3. Using the patterns provided, cut from orange wool: two beaks and four feet.
4. From green wool, cut seven strands, each 1/4" x 4", for hair.
5. From the batting, cut two wings.

Sew:
1. Sew the front belly to the back at the wide, curved ends, with right sides together. See Fig. 1.
2. With right sides together, sew the sides to the front and back. See Fig. 2. Leave the tail end open for turning.
3. Stuff the body and sew the opening closed.
4. Place the pairs of wings right sides together with a piece of batting on each pair. Sew around edges, leaving a small opening for turning. Turn to right side and stitch the opening closed.

5. Sew the tops of the wings to the sides of the body. This can be done by hand.
6. Place the pairs of foot pieces wrong sides together and sew a 1/4" seam around the outside of each one, leaving an opening for stuffing. Stuff them lightly and stitch the openings closed.
7. Sew the feet to the bottom of the penguin. This can be done by hand.
8. With wrong sides together, sew around the two sides of the beak with a 1/4" seam. Stuff the beak, turn under the raw edges of the open end, and sew to the penguin's face. Use the photo as a guide for placement.
9. Hand stitch the white eyes above the beak. Hand sew the eyeballs on the eyes.
10. Run a thread through one end of all seven green hair pieces. Gather them on the thread tightly to form a loose pom-pom. Sew to the top of the head. ✳

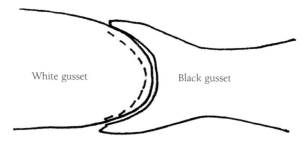

White gusset   Black gusset

Fig. 1 - Sewing the front white gusset to the black back gusset.

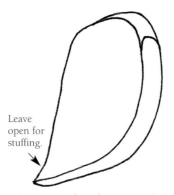

Leave open for stuffing.

Fig. 2 - Sewing the side pieces to the gusset.

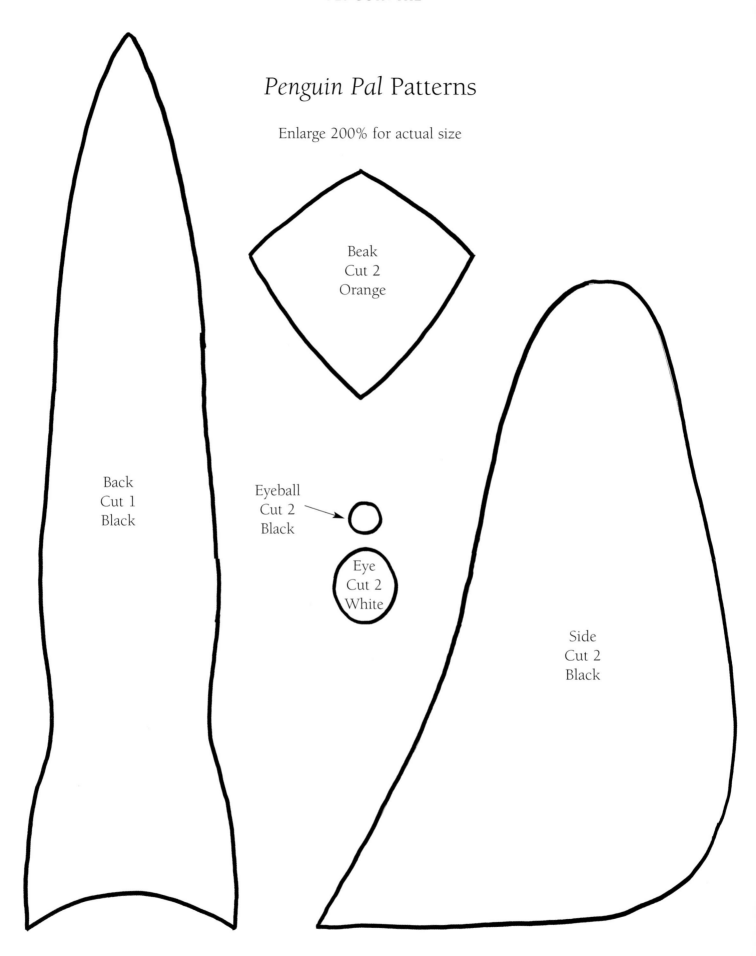

Penguin Pal Patterns

Enlarge 200% for actual size

Beak
Cut 2
Orange

Back
Cut 1
Black

Eyeball
Cut 2
Black

Eye
Cut 2
White

Side
Cut 2
Black

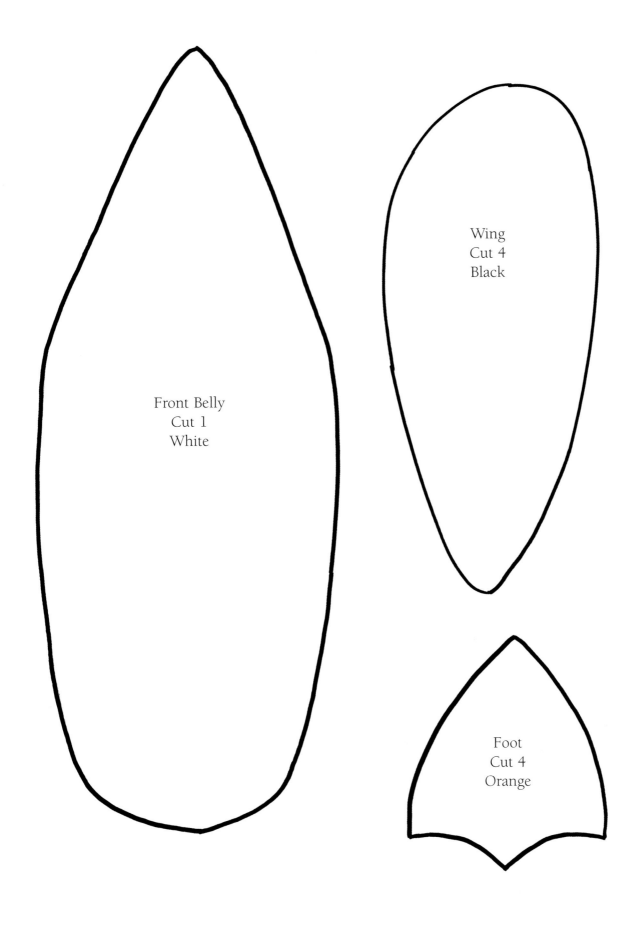

Front Belly
Cut 1
White

Wing
Cut 4
Black

Foot
Cut 4
Orange

Personalized Toy Crate

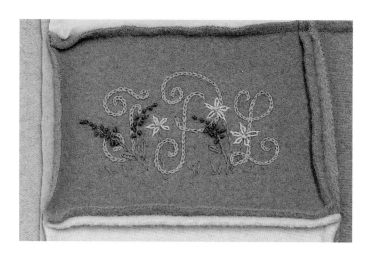

A colorful pieced wool cover turns an old wooden crate into a one-of-a-kind toy box for a child's room or the family room. You can use just about any type of wooden box or crate for the base. Paint it in a coordinating color and decorate with stencils, decals, or painted designs. The embroidered script monogram provides a personalized center for the pieced design.

SUPPLIES

Felted Wool:
- Lavender, 5-1/2" x 7-1/2"
- Pastel colors cut into strips 3" wide
- Lining piece, 22-1/2" x 17" (Choose a color to complement the top.)

Other Supplies:
- Wool tapestry yarn - Pink or blue, dark purple, lavender, white, yellow, green
- White sewing thread
- Wooden crate (Mine is 20" x 15".)
- 3/4" plywood, 21" x 15-1/2" or slightly larger than the top dimensions of the crate
- 4 wooden slats, 3/4" thick - Two 6" x 1-1/4", two 12" x 1-1/4"
- Foam rubber, 2" thick, 21" x 15-1/2"
- Spray foam adhesive
- Staple gun and staples
- Transfer paper and stylus
- Tracing paper and pencil
- Wood glue
- 8 nails, 1-1/4" long

INSTRUCTIONS

Make the Monogrammed Center Piece:
1. Construct a monogram of the child's initials by tracing letters from the script alphabet that appears on the following pages. Enlarge the letters so the center initial (for the last name) is 3" tall and the left initial (for the first name) and right initial (for the middle name) are 2" tall.
2. Transfer the letters to the center of the piece of lavender wool. Using the pattern provided, add the grass and flowers to the design.
3. Use one strand of wool yarn and a chain stitch to stitch the letters. (See the Basic Techniques section for Hand Embroidery instructions.)
4. Embroider the flowers and grass with wool yarn.

Piece the Cover:
All seams are 1/4" and on the right side of the fabric. All pieces except the center piece are strips 3" wide.
1. Start by sewing a strip to the bottom edge of the center piece. Trim the ends of the strip even with the center piece. See Fig 1.
2. Add second strip from the bottom edge of the first strip to the top of the center piece. See Fig. 1.
3. Add a third strip across the top. See Fig. 1.
4. Continue to add strips, following the sequence shown in Fig. 1, until you have a piece that is the size of the top of the foam piece. *continued on page 88*

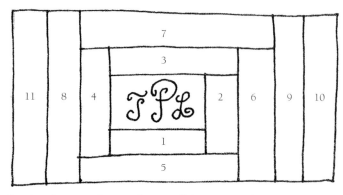

Fig. 1 - Placement diagram showing all the strips on the top.

continued from page 86

5. Use four more 3" wide strips for the sides. You may need to piece them to get the right length. See Fig. 2.

6. Make the bottom of the cover by sewing four 3" wide strips along the bottom edges of the side strips. See Fig. 3.

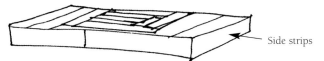

Fig. 2 - *Adding the side strips.*

Assemble the Top:

1. Spray the top of the plywood and the bottom of the foam with foam adhesive. Place the foam, glue side down, on top of the plywood.

2. Pull the cover over the foam-topped base. Use staples to secure it to the bottom of the plywood.

3. Place the piece of lining felt over the bottom, covering the plywood and the edges of the cover. Fold under the edges of the lining and staple securely to the wood.

4. Place the top on the crate to check the fit. Mark the placement for the slats, using Fig. 4 as a guide. (Mine are 1-1/2" inside the edges.) Nail the slats in place. Be sure the nails don't protrude through the foam. ✳

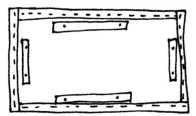

Fig. 3 - *Adding the bottom strips.*

Fig. 4 - *Placing the slats.*

Monogram Pattern

Actual size

Script Alphabet

Enlarge 200% for actual size

Initial Tote

This shopping bag is so handy and easy to make. You'll want to make a dozen of them to carry your groceries home. One side of the tote sports a monogram and the other side has a convenient outside pocket. Use the script alphabet on page 89 for a monogram pattern.

SUPPLIES

Felted Wool:
- Gray and white plaid (for front and back)
- Floral print (for sides and bottom)
- Striped wools (for monogram background, pocket flap, and frame)
- Red and black plaid (for button bases and handle)
- Plaid jacket pocket (for the back pocket)
- Black (for monogram)
- 1 sweater sleeve

Other Supplies:
- 4 silver buttons with shanks, 7/8"
- Heavy cardboard, 13" x 4-1/2"
- Water soluble stabilizer
- Black sewing thread

INSTRUCTIONS

Cut:

1. From the gray and white plaid, cut two pieces, each 14" square, for the front and back.

Other Side.

2. From the floral print, cut three pieces, each 14" x 6", for the side gussets and the bottom.
3. Cut a piece 9" tall and 8" wide with vertical stripes for the monogram patch.
4. Cut four frame strips 1-1/8" wide with crosswise stripes—two 13" long and two 11" long.
5. Cut the pocket from the plaid jacket, leaving 1/2" of extra fabric around pocket.
6. Cut four red 2" circles for button bases.
7. Cut two handles, each 6" x 16", from red and black plaid.
8. Cut a pocket flap 9" x 3". (Ribbing from bottom of sweater can be used for this.)

Instructions continued on page 92.

continued from page 90

9. Enlarge a letter from the script alphabet patterns on the previous pages or a letter from a font on your computer for the monogram. The letter should be 5-1/2" tall. Depending on the letter you choose, you may need to adjust the size of the wool strip. Mine was 6".

10. Cut a narrow strip of black felted wool 1/2" wide x the measured length for the letter. Or you can cut out a piece of wool the shape of your letter.

Attach the Monogram:

1. Pin the strip in the shape of the letter to the striped background.

2. Sew the letter to the striped background using a sewing machine and a zig-zag stitch.

Sew the Front & Back:

All seams are on the outside and 5/8" wide.

1. Place the striped piece with the monogram on the front of the tote. Using a straight stitch, sew it in place and free motion stitch all over the monogrammed piece to add texture.

2. Sew the 1-1/2" wide frame pieces to the sides of the monogram.

3. Cut a tiny hole at the center of each of the four 2" red circles large enough for a button shank to fit through. Push the shank of a button through the hole in each circle.

4. Position one felt circle on each corner of the frame. Sew the button shanks to the front.

5. Sew the pocket to the center of the back. Sew around pocket and again over the top stitching on the pocket. (If your pocket doesn't have top stitching, sew 1/4" inside the edge.)

6. Sew the pocket flap in place, overlapping the pocket.

Add the Gussets & Handles:

1. With right sides together, fold each side gusset piece in half lengthwise. Sew a 1/2" seam down the fold, 10" long, to make tucks in the side pieces and help the bag sit flat. See Fig. 1.

2. With wrong sides together, sew the back and front pieces to the side pieces.

3. With wrong sides together, sew the bottom to the front, the back, and the side gussets.

4. Fold the handle pieces in thirds so the handles are 2" wide.

5. Stitch several times along the length of each handle to reinforce it. Trim the edges. See Fig. 2.

6. With the raw ends inside, sew the handles to the bag. Slip the cardboard inside a felted sweater sleeve. Cut the sleeve to size so it covers the cardboard and sew the ends closed. Place in the bottom of the tote. ✳

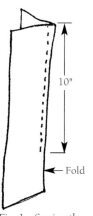

Fig. 1 - Sewing the gusset seam.

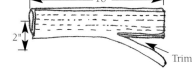

Fig. 2 - Trimming the edges of the handle.

Dowel Trivet

Cross stitch embroidery and scraps from seven felted sweaters are combined with wooden dowels to make this trivet. You can choose which side goes on top and which side is the bottom.

SUPPLIES

Felted Wool:
- 7 pieces of felted wool, each 2-1/2" x 6", in bright colors (I used red, mint green, red and orange striped, purple, orange, medium green, and mustard yellow.)

Other Supplies:
- 7 wooden dowels, 1/2" diameter, 6" long
- Wool tapestry yarn - Lime green, orange, yellow, gold, kelly green
- 4 yds. heavy cord (any color)
- 2 sewing needles, each 8" long

INSTRUCTIONS

1. Wrap each wool piece around a dowel, lining up the end of the wool and end of the wood. Trim off any excess wool.
2. Sew the seam shut with a cross stitch. See the Basic Techniques Section for cross stitch instructions. Choose contrasting colors, using the photo as a guide. (The ends of the dowels will show.)
3. Arrange the covered dowels in color order of your choice, with the cross stitched side on the bottom.
4. To connect the wrapped dowel pieces together, you will need to thread an 8" needle on each end of the 4-yd. length of cord. Use one needle to pull the

cord through the cover of the first dowel. Arrange the cord so that center of the cord is in the center of the first dowel cover and the ends are even.

5. Push one threaded needle through the second dowel cover. See Fig. 1. Then use the second threaded needle to push the other side of the cord through the second dowel cover from the opposite side. Pull tight. Keep going back and forth from one needle to the other until all of the dowel covers are connected. Tie off the cords and bury the ends under the last cover. ✶

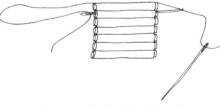

Fig. 1 - Connecting the dowels with cord.

Round Dog Bed

You can make this bed for a dog of any size. It's based on a circle divided into eight equal pieces. The instructions use the measurements for a small dog bed (a 30" circle). For larger dogs, use these sizes: for medium, a 36" circle; for large, a 42" circle; for extra large, a 48" circle. The cover zips off for easy cleaning.

SUPPLIES

Felted Wool:
- Assorted large pieces, including white or off-white

Other Supplies:
- 20" zipper
- 2 cotton fabric circles, 30" in diameter (for liner cushion)
- Stuffing material
- Sewing thread - White, black
- Kraft paper
- Pencil and ruler
- Sewing machine

INSTRUCTIONS

Cut:
1. On kraft paper, draw a 30" circle. Divide the circle into eight equal pieces. Cut out one piece to use as a pattern.
2. Using the pattern, cut eight pieces for the top of the bed and eight pieces for the bottom.
3. Using the pattern provided, cut out three bones from white or off-white wool. Set aside.

Sew:
1. With right sides together, sew all the pieces for the top together with 1/4" seams.
2. Using a straight stitch, attach the bones to the top, stitching 1/8" around the inside edge. See photo for placement of bones.
3. To make the bottom, sew two half-circles with four pieces each.
4. Connect the two halves of the bottom, adding a zipper between them, following the package instructions. See Fig. 1.
5. Place the top and bottom with right sides together, and sew around outside edge. Through the zipper opening, turn to right side.
6. With right sides together, sew the liner circles together, leaving an opening for turning. Turn, stuff, and sew the opening closed.
7. Place the liner cushion inside the dog bed cover. ✳

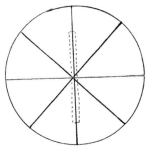

Fig. 1 - Placement of zipper in the bottom.

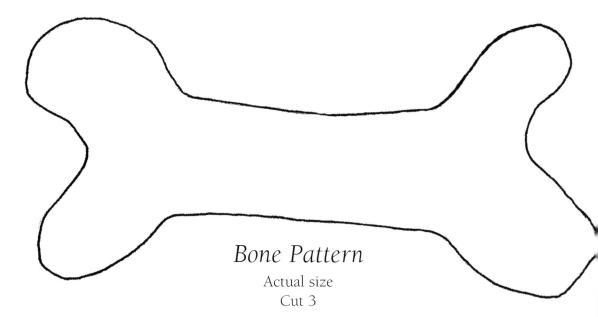

Bone Pattern
Actual size
Cut 3

Tea Cozy & Teapot Mat

This colorful cozy would make a great gift for a tea-drinking friend–the felted wool is a wonderful insulator. I've also included instructions for making a coordinated base pad that can be placed under the teapot.

SUPPLIES

Felted Wool:
- Red
- Scraps of mustard, lime green, grape

Other Supplies:
- Teapot
- Tape measure
- Wool tapestry yarn - Lime green, yellow, grape
- *Optional:* Sewing machine

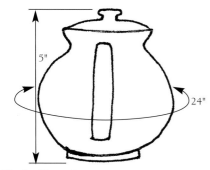

Fig. 1 - Measuring

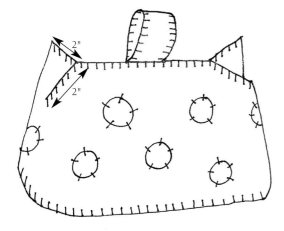

Fig. 2 - Sewing the top

INSTRUCTIONS

Make the Base Pad:
1. Cut one red 10" circle and one mustard 10" circle.
2. Stack them and blanket stitch around outside, joining the two layers with two strands of grape yarn.

Make the Cozy:
1. Measure the height of your teapot. (Mine was 5" tall.) Measure the circumference, around the widest point. (Mine measured 24".) See Fig. 1.
2. Cut a piece of red felt that is 1" longer than the circumference measurement. (I cut mine 25".) Make the width of the piece 3" taller than the height of the teapot (I cut mine 8".)
3. Cut four 1" circles of each color: mustard, grape, lime.
4. Position and pin them, randomly but evenly spaced, over the right side of the red felt piece.
5. Sew them to the red felt with five straight stitches, using two strands of yarn–yellow yarn on lime, lime yarn on grape, and grape yarn on mustard.
6. Join the two 8" ends of the red felt piece with a 1/4" seam. (You can use a sewing machine for this or stitch the seam by hand.)
7. With two strands of lime yarn, sew a blanket stitch around the bottom edge.
8. Cut a 2" x 7" piece of grape felt for the handle. Blanket stitch along both sides with two strands of lime yarn.
9. Position the seam on the cozy so it is at one of the sides. Fold the handle strip in half. Position and pin the handle at the center of the top, with the fold at top. Pin the top together, with the cut ends of the handle inside. Push the corners in so that you have 2" flaps on each side. Pin the entire top closed. Sew top closed with a blanket stitch and 2 strands of lime yarn. See Fig. 2.
10. *To use:* Place the teapot with hot water and tea inside on the round base pad. Cover it with the cozy. ✳

Leaves & Petals Table Runner

This attractive table runner is adorned with simple petal and leaf shapes cut from felted wool and joined by strands of yarn. Its border is a series of triangles that form a fringe.

Finished size: 20" x 76"

SUPPLIES

Felted Wool:
- Assorted pieces in grays and blacks, woven or knitted

Other Supplies:
- Black felt, 16" x 72"
- Wool tapestry yarn - Black
- Wool fettuccine-shaped yarn - Camouflage
- Water soluble stabilizer
- Black sewing thread
- Sewing machine
- Tracing paper and pencil
- Embroidery needle

INSTRUCTIONS

1. Cut and piece together eleven pieces of felted wool to form a rectangle 72" long and 16" wide. Overlap the pieces slightly.
2. Using stabilizer underneath and a machine overlock stitch, connect the overlapping edges of the runner.
3. Chain stitch stems in each section with three strands of black yarn, following the Placement Diagram. See the Basic Techniques section for chain stitching instructions.
4. Trace the patterns provided for the leaves and flower petals (pieces 1 through 5). Cut from black wool.

5. Hand sew the leaves and petals to the runner, using sewing thread and a simple straight stitch over the edges of each piece. See the Placement Diagram.
6. From black wool, cut long free-form leaf shapes for the center section of the runner, using the Placement Diagram as a guide. Straight stitch down the center of each.
7. From dark gray and light gray wool, cut triangles approximately 2" wide at the base and 2-1/2" tall for the fringe border.
8. Pin the triangles all around the edge of the runner, under the edge. Sew them in place with a zig-zag stitch 1/4" from the edge.
9. Place the black felt piece under the runner, with wrong sides together. (The felt piece will be larger than the runner.) Straight stitch along the zig-zag stitching in step 8.
10. Trim the felt 1/4" from the stitching line. ✳

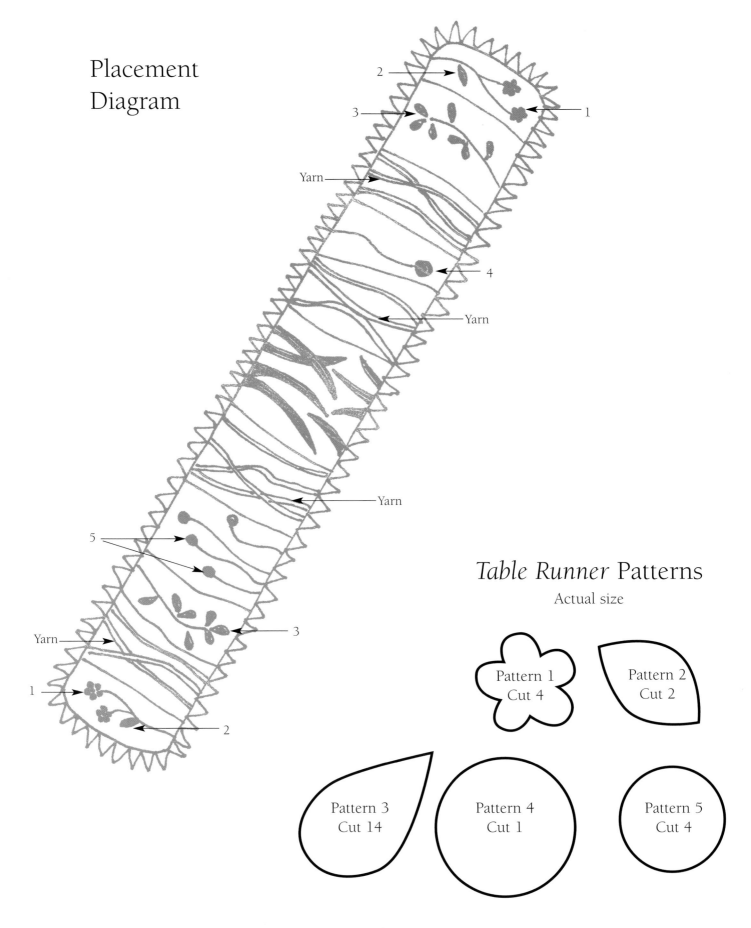

Placement
Diagram

2

3

1

Yarn

4

Yarn

Yarn

5

Yarn

3

1

2

Table Runner Patterns

Actual size

Pattern 1
Cut 4

Pattern 2
Cut 2

Pattern 3
Cut 14

Pattern 4
Cut 1

Pattern 5
Cut 4

Bull's Eye Trivet

The same coiling techniques used to make rugs can be applied to something smaller, like this trivet. This one is 8" in diameter.

SUPPLIES

Felted Wool:
- Sturdy pieces of purple, lime green, red, orange, and medium green

Other Supplies:
- Heavy duty sewing thread
- Sewing thread
- Tape measure

INSTRUCTIONS

Cut:
1. Cut a felted wool circle 7-1/2" in diameter. (This is the bottom.)
2. Cut the wool pieces into strips 1/2" wide.

Sew:
Sew the coils and wraps as you go, stitching through the middles of the sides of the strips. After the coil becomes too big to sew all the way through, just stitch through several layers. It's okay for the thread to show on the bottom of the trivet, but not on the top. Here's the sequence:
1. Using a strip of purple wool, roll a purple coil 1" in diameter.
2. Wrap a med. green strip around the purple center, making a 1/2" wide band.
3. Wrap a red strip next, making a 1" wide band of red felt.

4. Wrap a 1" wide band of orange felt.
5. Make a fan-folded wrap of lime green felt by running a needle and thread through the center of the green strip every 1". When you pull the thread tight, you will have a 1" wide fan fold. Make a piece long enough to wrap around the trivet (approximately 22").
6. Sew the fan-folded border around the trivet.

Cover the Bottom:
Sew the felt circle to the bottom of the trivet with sewing thread. ✳

Striped Pot Handle Cover

Wool is an excellent fabric to use in the kitchen because it's naturally flame resistant, and the dense texture of felted wool both insulates and protects. You can customize this pot handle cover to fit any saucepan or skillet handle.

SUPPLIES

Felted Wool:
• Very heavy (sturdy) green stripe
• Orange

Other Supplies:
• Plastic or metal ring, 1" diameter
• Large eye needle
• Wool tapestry yarn - Rust, lime green
• Sewing machine

INSTRUCTIONS

1. Measure the length of the handle. Subtract 1". This is the length to cut the piece of wool. Measure the circumference of the handle at its widest point. Add 1". This is the width to cut the wool. See Fig 1. For my pot, I cut a piece of striped green wool 7" x 4-1/2".

2. With wrong sides together, fold the handle cover in half lengthwise. Sew a 1/2" seam.

3. Using two strands of rust yarn, sew a blanket stitch down the seam. See Fig. 2.

4. Cut a piece of orange felt 4" x 1".

5. Blanket stitch both of the 4" sides with 2 strands of lime yarn.

6. Fold the orange felt piece in half over the 1" ring and push 3/4" into one end of the handle cover. Pin in place, centering the seam on the handle cover on one side. Blanket stitch the end with two strands of rust yarn. See Fig. 2.

To use: Slip onto pot handle.
To store: Hang from the ring. ✻

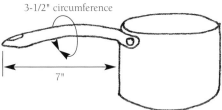

Fig. 1 - Measuring the handle of the pot.

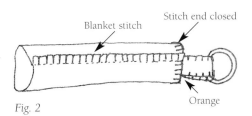

Fig. 2

Orange Pot Handle Cover

Pick a color that matches or contrasts with the color of your cookware—the choice is yours.

SUPPLIES
Felted Wool:
- Scraps of orange, yellow

Other Supplies:
- Wool tapestry yarn - Lime green
- Plastic or metal ring, 1"
- Sewing thread - Orange
- Sewing machine
- Tracing paper and pencil

INSTRUCTIONS
Cut:
1. Using the pattern provided, cut two handle covers from orange wool.
2. Cut 4" x 1" piece of yellow wool for the ring holder.

Assemble:
1. Push the yellow wool through the ring and fold the wool piece in half.
2. Insert 3/4" of the ends of the yellow wool piece between the pieces of the orange wool on the curved end.
3. Sew a 1/4" seam around the handle cover, leaving the straight end open.
4. Blanket stitch along the stitched sides and around the curved end with two strands of lime yarn.

To use: Slip onto pot handle.
To store: Hang from the ring. ✳

Pattern

Cut 2

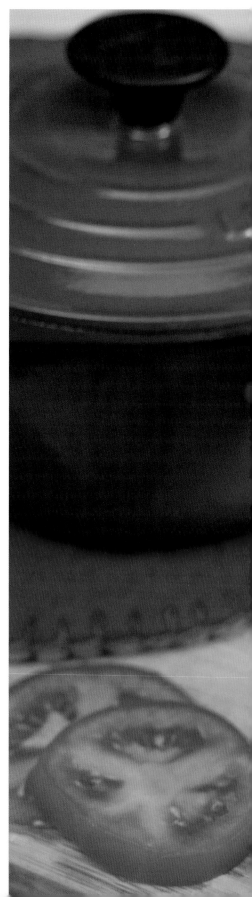

Fish Pot Handle Cover

Pattern on page 108.

This colorful fish will look great covering a pot handle or hanging on your kitchen wall.

SUPPLIES
Felted Wool:
• Scraps of mustard yellow, mint green

Other Supplies:
• Wool tapestry yarn - Orange, mint green
• Plastic or metal ring, 1" diameter
• 2 two-hole black buttons, 5/8"
• Sewing thread - Mustard yellow
• Sewing machine

INSTRUCTIONS
Cut:
1. Using the pattern provided, cut two fish bodies from mustard yellow.
2. Using the patterns, cut two tail pieces, two fin pieces, and two eyes from mint green.
3. From mustard yellow, cut a 1" x 3" piece for the ring holder.

Stitch the Fins, Tail, Eye, & Mouth:
See Fig. 1. See the Basic Techniques section for Hand Embroidery instructions.
1. Pin the green tail pieces and fins to the right sides of the fish body pieces.
2. Using one strand of orange yarn, stem stitch to secure the fins and tail pieces to the fish.
3. Pin the green eye pieces to the fish and stitch around each eye, using straight stitches.
4. Stem stitch the mouth.
5. Use green floss to sew a black button on each green eye.

Assemble:
1. Match the body pieces with wrong sides together. Machine sew around the fish bodies together, leaving the head area open to slip over pot handle. See Fig. 1.
2. Fold the ring holder piece in half, push it through the ring, and line up the ends. Push 3/4" of the ends between layers of the fish at the center of the tail.
3. With two strands of orange yarn, blanket stitch around each side of the open front end of the fish.
4. Around the rest of the fish (the part that has been sewn closed), blanket stitch through both layers.

To use: Push the open end of the fish over a pot handle.
To store: Hang from the ring. ✳

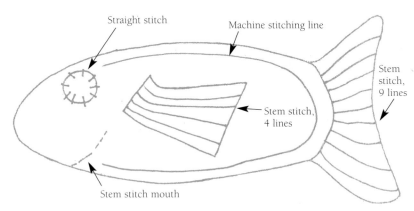

Fig. 1 - Stitching the fins, tail, eye, and mouth.

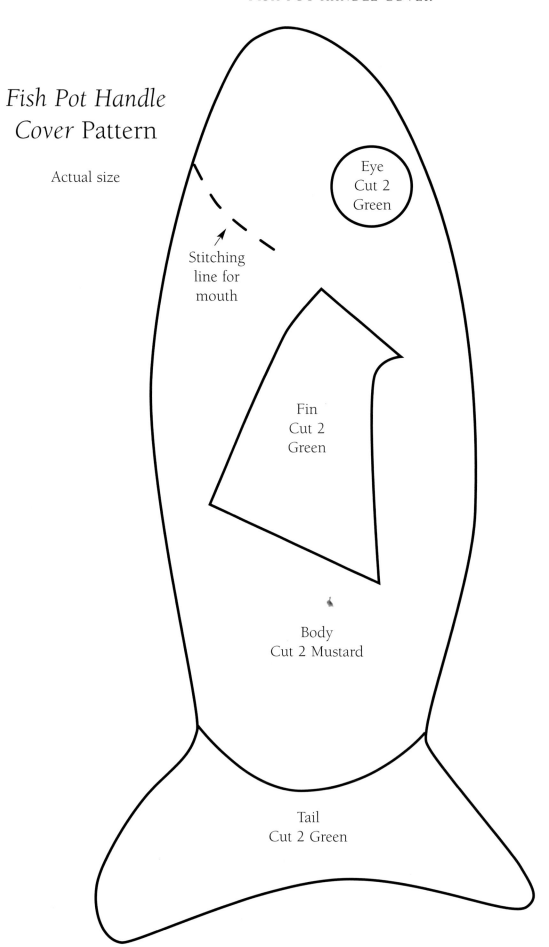

Fish Pot Handle Cover Pattern

Actual size

Stitching line for mouth

Eye
Cut 2
Green

Fin
Cut 2
Green

Body
Cut 2 Mustard

Tail
Cut 2 Green

Pictured opposite page: Color potholders or trivets are easy and fun to make. *Pictured clockwise from top:* Four Patch Square Pot Holder, Circles on a Circle Round Pot Holder, Paisley Pot Holder. Instructions begin on the next page.

Paisley Pot Holder

Layers of color and a distinctive shape make a useful, protective kitchen accessory. Use heavy, sturdy wool for pot holders.

SUPPLIES

Felted Wool:
- Scraps of orange, purple, yellow, red, lime green

Other Supplies:
- Wool tapestry yarn - Dark red, orange
- Plastic or metal ring, 1" diameter
- Sewing thread - Purple
- Tracing paper and pencil
- Sewing machine

INSTRUCTIONS

Cut:
1. Using the patterns provided, cut out all the pot holder pieces.
2. From red wool cut a 1" x 3-1/2" strip for the ring holder.

Sew:
1. Pin the flower center on the flower. Pin the flower with its center to the yellow shape. Blanket stitch around the flower center with two strands of orange yarn, attaching all three layers together.
2. Center the yellow felt piece to the purple felt piece and blanket stitch with two strands of dark red yarn.
3. Fold the 1" x 3-1/2" strip of red felt in half and push it through the ring. Align the ends and place it behind the orange scallop at the pointed end of the pot holder, leaving 1/2" of the folded end above the scallop.

4. Machine sew the purple piece to the orange scalloped piece, top stitching 1/4" in from the outside edge of the purple piece. (This also secures the ring holder to the pot holder.) Hand stitch the ends of the ring holder in place. ✳

Pattern

Actual size

Cut 1 of each piece

Orange

Purple

Yellow

Red

Green

Circles Pot Holder

Circles are stacked and sewn together, then accented with embroidery stitches. The finished pot holder is 8" in diameter.

SUPPLIES

Felted Wool:
- Scraps of red, mustard yellow, mint green, orange

Other Supplies:
- Wool tapestry yarn - Lime green, orange
- Plastic or metal ring, 1" diameter
- Sewing thread in colors to match wool
- Sewing machine
- Compass

INSTRUCTIONS

Cut:
1. From red, cut one 8" circle and one 1-1/2" circle.
2. From yellow, cut one 8" circle and one 1" x 3" yellow strip.
3. From green, cut one 6" circle.
4. From orange, cut one 2-1/2" circle.

Sew:
1. Place the red circle off center on the orange circle. Machine stitch 1/4" inside the edge of the red circle.
2. Place the orange circle 1" from one edge of the green circle. Machine stitch 1/4" inside the edge of the orange circle.
3. Place the green circle on the yellow circle. Machine stitch 1/4" from the outside edge of the green circle.
4. With three strands of orange yarn, straight stitch every 1/4" around the green circle.
5. Push the yellow strip through the ring and align the ends. Pin the ends of the strip behind the yellow circle.
6. Place the 8" red circle on the back of the pot holder, sandwiching the yellow ring holder between the red and yellow 8" circles. Machine stitch 1/4" from the outside edge.
7. With three strands of lime green yarn, straight stitch over the edge of the pot holder every 1/4". ✳

Four Patch Pot Holder

This four-patch pot holder is a good way to use up small scraps of felted wool. The finished size is 8" square.

SUPPLIES

Felted Wool:
- Solids - Purple, red, mint green, orange, olive green
- Stripes - Red and orange, green and blue

Other Supplies:
- Wool tapestry yarn - Lime green, dark red
- Plastic or metal ring, 1" diameter
- Sewing thread in colors to match wool
- Sewing machine

INSTRUCTIONS

Cut:
1. From purple, cut an 8" square.
2. Cut 4" squares from mint green, orange, red and orange stripes, and green and blue stripes.
3. From olive green, cut a 2-1/2" circle.
4. From red, cut a 1" x 4" strip for the ring holder.
5. Cut a 7-1/2" wool square to line the pot holder. This piece can be any color, since it will not show.

Sew:
1. Place the olive green circle in the center of the orange square. Machine stitch 1/4" inside the circle.
2. With three strands of lime green yarn, sew around the circle with straight stitches 1/4" apart.
3. Machine stitch the four 4" squares together with 1/4" seams on the outside.

4. Push the red 1" x 4" strip through the ring. Align the ends and pin them to the bottom of one corner of the patched square.
5. Place the 7-1/2" square behind the patched square. Put the purple square on the back. Sew around the outside edges of the pot holder 1/4" in from edge.
6. Use three strands of dark red wool yarn to blanket stitch around the entire square. ✳

Brown Bag It

Use this tan wool bag to hold paper for recycling–or carry your lunch to work in it. It will stand up and stay open, and you can use it again and again.

SUPPLIES

Felted Wool:
- Camel or tan (I used one skirt for all the pieces.)

Other Supplies:
- Brown wool tapestry yarn
- Pinking shears
- Water soluble marking pen
- Sewing thread to match wool
- Tracing paper and pencil
- Transfer paper and stylus
- Sewing machine

INSTRUCTIONS

Cut:
1. Cut two pieces, each 7" x 10", for the front and back.
2. Cut two sides, each 4" x 10".
3. Cut one piece 7" x 4" for the bottom.

Assemble:
1. Mark folding lines in the two side pieces with a water soluble marking pen. See Fig. 1.
2. Fold the pieces along the guidelines with right sides together and sew a 1/8" seam along all three fold lines on the inside of the bag.
3. Using the pattern provided, transfer the word "paper" to the bag, placing it 4" above the bottom of the front piece.
4. Using one strand of tapestry yarn and a stem stitch, embroider the letters.
5. With wrong sides together, sew the sides to the front and back pieces, making 1/4" seams. Sew the bottom piece to the bottom edges, using a 1/4" seam allowance.
6. Trim the top of the bag with pinking shears.
7. Cut a 1" diameter half circle at the center top of the front and back. ✳

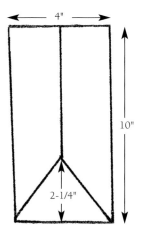

Fig. 1 - Folding lines on side pieces.

Lettering Pattern

Actual size

paper

Striped Tassel

The striped and patterned sleeve bottom of a felted Fair Isle sweater makes a colorful tassel.

SUPPLIES

Felted Wool:
- Sweater sleeve with horizontal stripes, 8" long
- Scraps of wool from the same sweater as the sleeve

Other Supplies:
- 3 round wooden beads, 3/4"
- Acrylic craft paints–Pink, lime green, dark blue
- 20" green grosgrain ribbon with blue dots, 7/8" wide
- Heavy-duty thread or cord (for gathering)
- Paint brushes
- Long hook or bodkin

INSTRUCTIONS

1. Cut one end of the sleeve into fringe 1/2" wide and 4-1/2" long.
2. Sew a gathering cord around the top of the fringed part and pull tight. See Fig 1.
3. Sew a second gathering cord along the top edge of the sleeve piece. Turn down the top of the sleeve, with the wrong side of the sleeve showing, and pull tight. See Fig 2. The second gathering cord should cover the first gathering cord.
4. Cut six 1" squares from the sweater scraps. Cut slits in the centers of all the 1" squares.
5. Paint two wooden beads with pink paint. Paint the other wooden bead with lime green paint. Let dry. Paint blue dots on the lime green bead. Let dry.
6. Fold the ribbon in half. Cut the ends at a slant. Using a long hook or bodkin, pull the ends of the ribbon through a pink bead, leaving a loop for hanging.
7. Thread three squares on the ribbon ends.
8. Pull the ribbon ends through the green dotted bead.
9. Add the three remaining squares and one pink bead. Adjust the ribbon so the hanging loop above the first bead is 3".
10. Pull the ends of the ribbon through the top of the tassel. Tie the ribbon ends into a really big knot so they can't come back out. Trim the ends. ✳

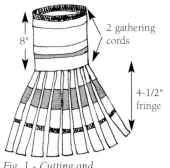

Fig. 1 - Cutting and gathering diagram.

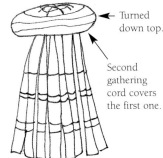

Fig. 2 - Forming the top of the tassel.

Gray & Green Tassel

Glass beads in silver and green add sparkle and shine to a tassel made from a sweater sleeve.

SUPPLIES

Felted Wool:
• Sleeve from a gray print sweater

Other Supplies:
• 33 silver seed beads
• 235 silver-lined lime green seed beads
• Lime green bead, 3/4" x 1"
• 1-1/2 yds. silver wire, 26 gauge
• Needlenose pliers

INSTRUCTIONS

1. From the sweater sleeve, cut six strips 3/4" wide and 12" long.
2. On a 12" piece of wire, thread 33 silver seed beads. Fold this wire in half with the beads at the folded end. Twist the wire ends together under the beads to form a loop. See Fig 1.
3. Run both wires through the large green bead.
4. Fold the wool strips in half lengthwise. Bring them together at the center fold on the wire. Secure the ends of the wire underneath the fold.
5. Thread all of the green seed beads on the remaining piece of wire.
6. Hold the wool strips 1" below the fold and wrap rows of beads tightly around the tassel. See Fig. 2. Secure the ends of the wire and trim. ✳

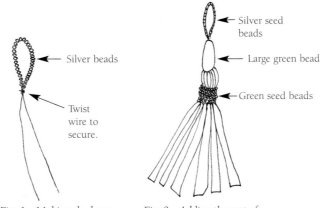

Fig. 1 - Making the loop for hanging.

Silver beads

Twist wire to secure.

Silver seed beads

Large green bead

Green seed beads

Fig. 2 - Adding the rest of the beads.

Utility Bin Cover

Felted wool makes a sturdy, colorful cover for a wire-frame utility bin. The bins can be used for storing all kinds of items, from clothes and diapers to mail and reading material. I've included a variety of label and applique designs for stylish sorting and storage. The appliques indicate what is in the bin; the label holder provides a space for labeling what is inside the bin.

SUPPLIES

Felted Wool:

- Colors of your choice

Other Supplies:

- Canvas-covered wire frame utility bin, 10" wide x 13" deep x 7-1/2" high
- 44" hook-and-loop fastener tape (You'll only use the hook side.)
- Sewing machine

INSTRUCTIONS

1. Remove the canvas covering from the bin. Keep the wire frame and bottom insert. See Fig. 1.
2. From wool, cut two sides, each 14" x 10".
3. Cut two ends, each 10" square.
4. Cut one bottom piece, 12" x 9".
5. Pin the bottom, sides, and ends, with right sides out, to the wire frame. **Note:** Because the bin is smaller at the bottom than at the top, there will be excess wool along the bottoms of the sides.
6. Remove the fabric from the bin. Sew along the pinned lines, sewing the corner seams only to the top bar of the bin (7-1/2"). Trim all seams to 1/4".
7. Trim the corners as shown in Fig. 2.
8. Sew the hook portion of the hook-and-loop fastener tape to each side along the inside top. (Since the hook tape will attach to the wool, you don't need the loop side.)
9. Place the cover on the frame and fold the in top edges, securing the cover to the frame.
10. Cut two pieces of wool slightly larger than the bottom insert. Sandwich the insert between the two pieces of wool and sew around the outside, enclosing the insert. Put the wool-covered insert in bottom of bin.
11. Add a label window or applique. See the following pages for instructions and photos. ✳

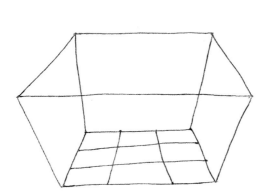

Fig. 1 - The wire-frame bin.

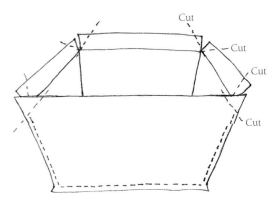

Fig. 2 - Trimming the corners.

Utility Bin Label Holder

Pictured on page 119.

SUPPLIES

Felted Wool:
- Color of your choice, 3-1/2" x 4-1/2"

Other Supplies:
- Heavy clear vinyl, 5" x 7"
- Tracing paper and pencil
- Card stock (to make a label)
- Fine tip marker
- Sewing machine

INSTRUCTIONS

1. Using the pattern, cut out the wool for the label holder. Cut out the center area.
2. Place the vinyl under the felted wool. (It will be larger than label holder.) Top stitch 1/8" from the window opening.
3. Sew a line of top stitching on left side only, 1/4" from the first line of stitching. (This side will be left open to insert a label.) See Fig. 1.
4. Trim vinyl so it is 1/8" smaller than the label holder.
5. Pin the label holder to one end of the bin cover. Top stitch the three other sides (top, right, and bottom) 1/4" from the first line of stitching.
6. Cut a label and write the name of the bin contents with a marker. Insert the label in the label holder. ✳

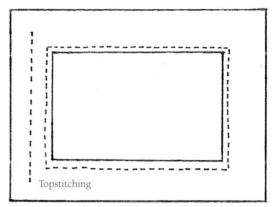

Topstitching

Fig. 1 - Stitching diagram.

Pattern   Actual size

Flower Label Holder Pattern

Instructions appear on page 122.

Actual size

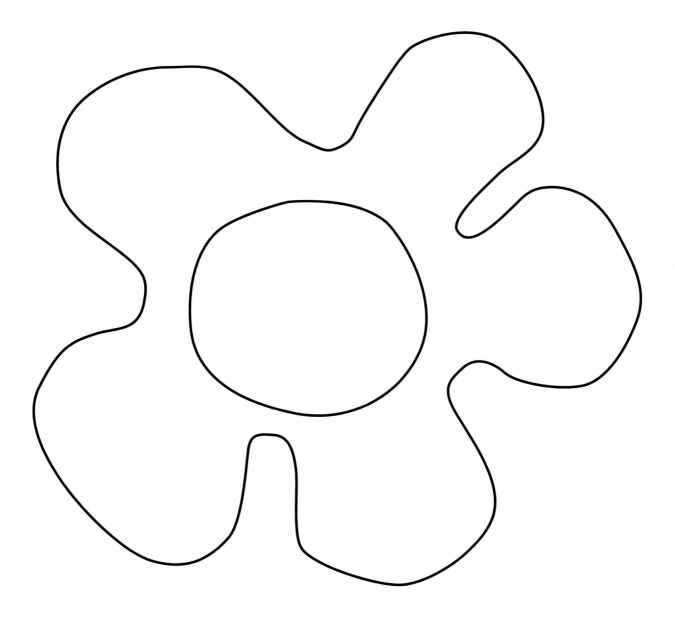

Flower Label Holder

Here is an alternative label holder for a utility bin. Cover a wire frame utility bin with felted wool using the instructions given on page 118.

Pattern appears on page 121.

SUPPLIES

Felted Wool:
• Scrap in any flower color

Other Supplies:
• Heavy duty vinyl, 8" square
• 2 heavy duty, industrial strength adhesive-backed hook & loop dots (You'll only use the hook side.)
• Sewing thread to match wool
• Sewing machine
• Card stock (to make a label)
• Fine tip marker

INSTRUCTIONS

1. Using the pattern provided, cut out the flower. Cut away the center of the flower.
2. Place the flower cutout on the vinyl square. Topstitch 1/16" from the flower center. See Fig. 1. Topstitch again 1/4" from the previous topstitching.
3. Topstitch 1/8" inside the top edge of the flower to make the opening for the label to be inserted. See Fig. 1. Trim the vinyl even with the edge of the flower.

4. Place the flower on one end of the utility bin cover. To attach, sew around the edge of the flower except in the area that was topstitched in step 3.
5. Put the hooked half of a hook & loop dot on the upper petals, which are not sewn to the cover. See Fig. 2.
6. Cut a label from card stock. Write the name of the contents on the label. Insert the label in the label holder. ✳

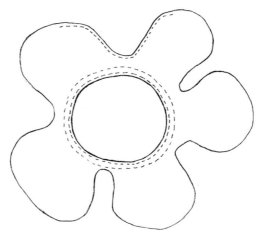
Fig. 1 - Stitching diagram.

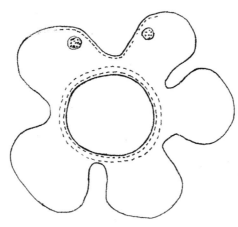
Fig. 2 - Placement diagram for hook & loop dots.

Diaper Applique

Use this cute diaper appliqué on the front of a wool-covered utility bin to hold baby diapers or other infant essentials. Cover a wire frame utility bin with felted wool using the instructions given on page 118.

SUPPLIES

Felted Wool:

• Scrap of white

Other Supplies:

• Large diaper pin
• Sewing thread - White
• Tracing paper and pencil

INSTRUCTIONS

1. Using the pattern provided, cut out the diaper.
2. Fold in the sides of the diaper. Fold up the center. Fold the point of the center piece over the top of the diaper front. Secure in place by sewing with white thread.
3. Add the pin to the front of the diaper.
4. Sew to the front of the utility bin. ✽

Pattern

Actual size

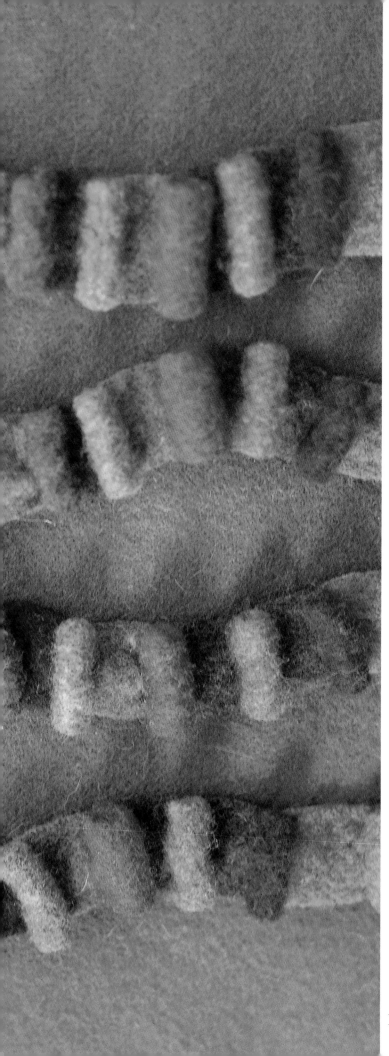

Metric Conversion Chart

Inches to Millimeters and Centimeters

Inches	MM	CM
1/8	3	.3
1/4	6	.6
3/8	10	1.0
1/2	13	1.3
5/8	16	1.6
3/4	19	1.9
7/8	22	2.2
1	25	2.5
1-1/4	32	3.2
1-1/2	38	3.8
1-3/4	44	4.4
2	51	5.1
3	76	7.6
4	102	10.2
5	127	12.7
6	152	15.2
7	178	17.8
8	203	20.3
9	229	22.9
10	254	25.4
11	279	27.9
12	305	30.5

Yards to Meters

Yards	Meters
1/8	.11
1/4	.23
3/8	.34
1/2	.46
5/8	.57
3/4	.69
7/8	.80
1	.91
2	1.83
3	2.74
4	3.66
5	4.57
6	5.49
7	6.40
8	7.32
9	8.23
10	9.14

Index

A
Appliqued Chair Cover 46
Appliqued Placemat 58

B
Bag 114
Batting 82
Bead(s) 14, 116, 117
Bear 76
Bin cover 118
Blanket 64
Boo Boo Toy 80
Bottle cover 70, 72
Brown Bag It 114
Brush 36, 116
Bull's Eye Trivet 102
Button(s) 15, 42, 76, 90, 106

Cardboard 90
Cardstock 120, 122
Chair cover 46, 51
Chair Seat Cushion 50
Chalk 30, 31
Circles of Cuffs Pillow 31
Circles Pot Holder 112
Coiled Oval Rug 60
Compass 112
Cord 64, 93, 116
Cotton 94
Crate 86
Crazy Quilt Trunk Top 36
Cuddly Brown Bear 76
Cutting 19
Cutting mat 12

D
Diaper Applique 124
Diaper pin 124
Dog bed 94
Dowel Trivet 93
Dowels 93

E
Edges 21
Embellishments 14

F
Felt 98
Felted wool, creating 18
Fish Pot Handle Cover 106
Fleece 64
Floss, embroidery 15
Flower Cuts Rug 52
Flower Label Holder 122
Foam
  adhesive 86
  pad 50
  rubber 36, 86
Four Patch Pot Holder 113

G
Glue 36, 86
Gray & Green Tassel 117

H
Hammer 36
Heart Hot Water Bottle Cover 70
Hook 116
Hook-and-loop dots 122
Hook-and-loop fastener tape 118
Hot water bottle 70, 72

I
Initial Tote 90

L
Label holder 120, 122
Lamb Hot Water Bottle Cover 72
Leaves & Petals Table Runner 98
Loopy Stripes Pillow 32
Lumber 36
Flowered Slippers 78

M
Marker 120, 122
Metal ring 103, 104, 106, 110, 112, 113
Monogrammed Chair Cover 51

N
Nails 36, 86
Needle(s) 14
  embroidery 98
  hand-sewing 14, 60, 76, 93
Nine-Dot Pillow 30

O
Orange Pot Handle Cover 104
Ottoman 42

P
Paint 36, 116
Paisley Pot Holder 110
Paper 94
Pattern(s) 16, 27, 40, 41, 44, 45, 54, 55, 56, 57, 68, 69, 71, 74, 75, 78, 79, 84, 85, 88, 89, 94, 100, 105, 108, 111, 120, 121, 125
Pen(s) 16, 114
Pencil(s) 16, 42, 52, 76, 80, 82, 86, 94, 98, 104, 114, 120, 124
Penguin Pal 82
Personalized Toy Crate 86
Pillow 28, 30, 31, 32, 34
Pink Fringed Pillow 28
Placemat 58
Pliers, needlenose 16, 117
Plywood 36, 86
Pot handle cover 103, 104, 106
Pot holder 110, 112, 113
Primrose Path Throw 24
Projects 23
Purple Flower Stool 38

R

Reupholstered Round Ottoman 42
Ribbon 70, 72, 116
Rotary cutters 12
Round Dog Bed 94
Rug 52, 60, 62
Ruler 12, 94

S

Scalloped Edge Rug 62
Scissors 12
Seam ripper 13
Seat cushion 50
Sewing 19
Sewing machine 13, 24, 28, 31, 32, 34,
    38, 42, 46, 50, 52, 58, 62, 64, 70, 72,
    76, 80, 82, 90, 94, 96, 98, 103, 104,
    106, 110, 112, 113, 114, 118, 120,
    122
Shears 114
Stabilizer 13, 24, 38, 50, 58, 62, 76, 80,
    90, 98
Staple gun 36, 38, 42, 86
Staples 36, 38, 42, 86
Stitches 21
Stool 38
Striped pot Handle Cover 103
Striped Tassel 116
Stuffing 76, 80, 82, 94

Stylus 86, 114
Supplies
    general 10
    miscellaneous 16
    sewing 13
Sweater(s), general information 11
Sweet Dreams Baby Blanket 64

T

Table runner 98
Tape measure 13, 46, 50, 96, 102
Tassel 116, 117
Tea Cozy & Teapot Mat 96
Teapot 96
Techniques, basic 17
Thirty-two Squares Pillow 34
Thread(s) 13, 15, 24, 28, 30, 31, 32,
    34, 38, 42, 46, 50, 52, 58, 60, 62, 64,
    70, 72, 76, 80, 82, 86, 90, 94, 98,
    102, 104, 106, 110, 112, 113, 114,
    122, 124
Throw 24
Tools
    cutting 12
    sewing 13
Tote 90
Toy 80
Tracing paper 42, 46, 52, 76, 80, 82,
    86, 98, 104, 110, 114, 120, 124

Transfer paper 16, 86, 114
Trivet 93, 102
Trunk top 36

U

Utility Bin Label Holder 120

V

Vinyl 120, 122

W

Wire 14, 117
Wood slats 86
Wool, felted 24, 28, 30, 32, 34, 36, 38,
    42, 46, 50, 52, 58, 60, 62, 64, 70, 72,
    76, 80, 82, 86, 90, 93, 94, 96, 98,
    102, 103, 104, 106, 110, 112, 113,
    114, 116, 117, 118, 120, 122, 124

Y

Yarn(s) 15
    knitting 15
    wool 15, 24, 36, 38, 62, 64, 70, 72,
    76, 86, 93, 96, 98, 103, 104, 106,
    110, 112, 113, 114

Z

Zipper 94